OUR HEART'S DESIRE

is our

LITTLEST MIRACLE

"THE CALLING"

A TESTIMONY OF SETH G. WHARTON

SETH G. WHARTON
BENAY WHARTON

XULON PRESS

Xulon Press
2301 Lucien Way #415
Maitland, FL 32751
407.339.4217
www.xulonpress.com

Unless otherwise indicated, Scripture quotations taken from the New King James Version (NKJV). Copyright © 1982 by Thomas Nelson, Inc. Used by permission. All rights reserved.

Scripture quotations taken from the King James Version (KJV) – *public domain.*

Scripture quotations taken from the Holy Bible, New International Version (NIV). Copyright © 1973, 1978, 1984, 2011 by Biblica, Inc.™. Used by permission. All rights reserved.

Paperback ISBN-13: 978-1-66285-953-3
Hard Cover ISBN-13: 978-1-66285-954-0
Ebook ISBN-13: 978-1-66285-955-7

Table of Contents

Chapter 1: The First Signs & First Attacks. 1

Chapter 2: Precious Memories 12

Chapter 3: Lessons From God 31

Chapter 4: Accusations Through Preparations 44

Chapter 5: Finding The Right One 65

Chapter 6: First Assignments Ministry: Planting The
             Church & Birth of SWMI 77

Chapter 7: From Generation to Generation: Seeing The
             Spirit Fall On Our Kids. 107

Section 2: A Little Bit More: "Then Came Seth" 139

Section 3: The Baptism of The Holy Spirit: Receiving,
             Praying & Using 151

Our Heart's Desire
is
Our Littlest Miracle
Part III
"The Calling"
Seth Wharton
Benay Wharton

"I want my life to be full of God's divine hand, and it is amazing what God will do when you answer "The Call" and say... "Not my will, but Your will be done!" -Seth Wharton

"There is a beautiful awareness of the "Touch of Jesus" in one's life when completely leaning upon Him." -Benay Wharton

I dedicate this book to:

My Lord and Savior, Jesus, who saved me. Who spared and has blessed my life. To my parents and the price they paid, in prayer and everything. And to my wife and kids, who I am so proud of. A lasting testimony and memorial of what The Lord has done for us. And to you, the reader. May it bless, encourage and draw you closer to Him! To know that in everything, God is good!

Foreword By Benay Wharton

$\mathcal{T}$he Journey of a little miracle baby with heart problems to an anointed called minister of God. Confirmed by word and spirit when Seth was a teenager, to us his parents that he was appointed. It was a powerful night we will never forget in our rooms as we settled into bed. The Lord showed up with the word for Seth, "APPOINTED" 2nd Timothy 1:11-12: When Paul says, *"Whereunto I am appointed a preacher, and an apostle and a teacher."* We have seen first hand how the tiny hands and feet of a small baby born with heart problems grew to be used of God as a preacher, an apostle and a teacher. Where now his adult hands through God appointment, reaches many hearts and souls. Where his adult feet take him into every culture, religion, race to tell the good news, Jesus Saves. We have seen Seth's family grow into his ministry, with his wife Kendra who's heart is to worship God and be in complete unity with her husband in his ministry calling. His children, Sarah, Isaiah, Rachel and Hannah, all have been blessed with spiritual giftings and a boldness to tell the good news. In this day and time, how wonderful and refreshing to see God work through these children who just add to the richness and power of Seth's ministry.

We have been there as we watched and prayed through every obstacle, heartache, victory, testimony and yes have seen the favor of God and man on his life. We have seen how God has turned what the enemy would use to defeat his ministry, into one victory after another, with signs and miracles following. This is his personal story, that takes you through the hard, yet successful journey of being truly "called" of God. We have witnessed and been in the shadows praying for this little miracle baby who has become God's hands and feet here on earth. We have seen first hand the many events, obstacles and miracles that Seth G. Wharton delicately, emotionally and discretely, yet without reservation, tells the story of his unique call and walk with God. Be prepared to be amazed, surprised and encouraged. That what God can do for Seth, God can do for you.

Please embrace this true account of Seth's walk with God, as witnessed by us, and can verify and confirm Seth's heart and love of God, his purpose…to only do God's will.

This is a poem my Dad (Seth's Grandfather) wrote to Seth.
It speaks volumes and I wanted to share it.

Seth

On top a rugged mountain
Buried 'neath the melting snow
A tiny little acorn
Taking root began to grow.

In its battle for survival

Its growth was very slow
Until its roots were anchored
In the depth of earth below.

It grew to be a living giant
Proudly standing straight and tall
Like a sentinel on the skyline
Summer, winter, spring and fall.

You have a lot in common
With the life of that big tree
Having had a rough beginning
Then what you turned out to be.

From that little fallen acorn
Came a work of God to see
And you became a lighthouse
On the shore beside the sea.

All things are for a purpose
As it was meant to be
You have a higher calling
Reaching souls in jeopardy.

A tree can't offer any hope
To sinners far and wide
But you can beam a ray of light
To those drifting on life's tide.

I'm blessed in having seen you
Grow up before my eyes
With a sense of righteous values
You will not compromise.

By Shirl A. Higgs

Our Heart's Desire

Is

Our Littlest Miracle

Part III

"The Calling"

Introduction

I had always felt "Called" from the time I was little. But it wasn't until about the age of 16 that the official "Call" had come. I had signs leading up to a day, when I was 16, sitting in my chemistry class, when God spoke to me. He said, "I really want to use you…" And as I felt the presence of the Lord and as tears came down my face I was thankful. God then said, "But, you are going to have to go through it, first…." I knew He meant suffering…I knew He meant to pick up the Cross…To count the cost first…And then I also knew He was waiting on my answer… My reply…and with tears…not knowing what others might have thought in my class…It was just me and The Lord…I said, "Lord, I don't want to have to go through it…but, not my will…but Your will be done." I did not know …at the time what, "through it" meant… but I would soon learn…the Great Price of Truly being "Called" by God!

Through false accusations, betrayal and many mighty words and miracles of God, *That will just amaze you*. This book is guaranteed to explode your faith, open your eyes and see what it is to be truly "Called" and used by God. The Price of following Jesus Christ into His Perfect will and the Blessings there are in trusting God through the fire.

Preface

s I went on from growing up with heart issues, (3 open heart surgeries, 6 cardiac catheterizations, S.B.E.-Subacute Bacterial Endocarditis...which is a deadly disease & 5 blood clots, see "Our Heart's Desire is Our Littlest Miracle" Part II, (another book) which is mostly the first 13yrs of my life.) and as God started to show His calling on my life, little did I know, the battles yet to come would be worse, longer in duration and harder than anything I had been through physically. It was the unseen spiritual battles, and the stripping down and purifying of the fire. The undercut of the suffering I was in, being discredited, dishonored, and betrayed. Undercut of what I had been through, and going through, the devil and devilish people trying to steal, kill and destroy my calling and testimony, even my very life. Being blamed instead of honored for the demonic assault, "How can God deliver me? How could I be healed of such attacks? How is this God?" Where do you turn? In the midst of it all, God can turn everything meant for evil, for good. Everything meant for loss, for gain. Those things meant to destroy you being used to promote and bless you. In the end, saying " Like Joseph, Genesis 50:20 *"But as for you, you meant evil against me; but God meant it for good, in order to bring it about as it is this day, to save many people alive."* What the devil meant for evil God used for good. Rejected into God's plan, betrayed into God's calling and promotion. Only God can do preparation for the promotion, high calling and to be set apart. To be set apart is not easy but hard training to handle the hard calling. To stay Holy and Humble so it doesn't destroy you, when promotion comes. Skip the price and you miss the power of God and for it to be real ministry.

I'm talking about a "True Calling" from God.

Chapter 1

The First Signs & First Attacks

(Not my will but Your will be done)

As I prayed in class and felt The Spirit of God, with tears coming down my face, God said, "I want to use you, but you're going to have to go *through it* first." And God waited for my reply...

Up until then I had always felt "Called". I always felt everyone just knew it, that I was "Called" and could feel it. It was just on me. I had signs earlier at a kids' camp, where the lessons & signs of God started. Through attack, a lot of times, is when the power of God will fall. I was starting to have trouble with some friends, who I felt were not treating me right. I said, "Well, I will just hang out and make other friends." That night was the first night I remember it so vividly. (For some reason the things of God, miracles and special things, I can recall so vividly.) As I was overcoming the hurt by friends, I remember going to pray in the back room and some of my new friends were there seeking to be baptized in The Holy Spirit, which is for All of us. Acts 2:38 says, *"Then Peter said to them, "Repent, and let every one of you be baptized in the Name of Jesus Christ for the remission of sins; and you shall receive the gift of The Holy Spirit. For this promise is to you and to your children, and to all who are afar off, as many as The Lord our God will call."*

Somehow I got praying for this new friend and suddenly he received the baptism of The Holy Spirit. He then went and got our two other new friends, and said, "Meet my new friend. He just prayed with me and I was filled with The Holy Spirit." SO... they also wanted me to pray with them. And would you believe it...They were baptized in The Holy Spirit with the evidence of speaking in tongues. (cannot be taught, just received) Powerful! I did not know then but would come to know later, that around the time of God moving in power, there is a price to pay. So you can handle it right and that He gets all the Glory. People today are taught to avoid The Cross & suffering. That is why there is no power. Just an outward appearance, an act, a form of godliness but denying The Power. "For the message of the cross is foolishness to those who are perishing, but to us who are being saved it is the power of God." 1 Corinthians 1:18

People think that it's an honor to have everyone like you when you are in the ministry. Although, I feel you can have Godly favor, but beware, the Bible says when everyone likes you, it's false. Luke 6:26 says, *"Woe to you when all men speak well of you, for so did their fathers to the false prophets."* And John 5:41-44 says, *"I do not receive honor from men. But I know you, that you do not have the love of God in you. I have come in My Father's Name, and you do not receive Me; if another comes in his own name, him you will receive. How can you believe, who receive honor from one another, and do not seek the honor that comes from the only*

God?" The kids ended up sharing to the group what God did and said, "I was a great friend." God has a way of putting the truth out there...and if God be for me who can be against me?

As that week concluded, our counselor was saying goodbye to everyone, praying for each one. When He came to me he said, *"I feel God is going to use others, but I really feel He is going to use you and I am not saying that to the others."* Needless to say, that got my attention. A few months later I received a word, when we were visiting a church. At the altar time, the one ministering gave a word saying, *"There is someone here The Lord is really going to use."* It went on for a little while... as I prayed... "Lord, if it's me you're going to use, I have to know, confirm it if it's me...." He said, *"You are wondering if it's you or not..."* As I was about to get up and go back to my seat....I heard, "Seth, will you come up here?" I was then called up in front of the church to be prayed over. With the one ministering saying they feel God is really going to use me, that it was me the word was for. I was amazed and felt God had confirmed the word. I would later go on, as I grew and matured in The Lord, to learn, that even some of the ones God would use to speak to me, would later betray me. I would wonder why or how that could be? God sometimes uses people to show them that God is with me and even from their own lips give testimony to it. And everyone has choices, like King Saul to David. Even when King Saul was trying to kill David, He testified saying, He knows God was going to use him and that he is going to do great things. 1 Samuel 24:17-21 says, *"Then he said to David; "You are more righteous than I, for you have rewarded me with good, whereas I have rewarded you with evil. And you have shown this day how you have dealt well with me; vs. 19 "Therefore may The Lord reward you with good for what you have done to me this day. And now I know indeed that you shall surely be king, and that the kingdom of Israel shall be established in your hand."*

After these signs, within a couple months of each other, that no one knew of the other, this led up to The Question God would ask me in class...

I also would come to learn, that even when God uses someone to speak through and to you, doesn't always mean later, they will be for you. Even when God has confirmed The "Calling" through them & to them, like King Saul to David, he knew God was with David. He went against him instead of being with him. And really that attack is actually confirmation that you are "Called". Like Joseph, I always felt like if it would be my family truly "Called", I would love it. To be with them & for them. I would not be against them, jealous of them, and try to stop or steal their calling. In which no one can steal a calling. Whatever is allowed by God works for His plan, but it's not OK for the ones that go against it. If you go against and fight against, who God has "Called", you will pay for it. It will work out for God's perfect plan, for those God has "Called". Even David would not touch God's Anointed, even when King Saul was in the wrong. There may be times to stand, but be careful.

May everyone see & know, what it is to have a true "Calling". Many want to just go into ministry but you can not take this honor upon yourself. Hebrews 5:4 says, *"And no man takes this honor to himself, but he who is CALLED by God, just as Aaron was."* Self-called, self-promoting ministers and ministries, that is what has led to the powerless ministries deceiving people away from

4

true repentance and true salvation power. To give them "another" way, a way around the cross, complete surrender and suffering. Jesus said, *"If anyone desires to come after Me, let him deny himself, and take up his cross, and follow Me. For whoever desires to save his life will lose it, but whoever loses his life for My sake will find it."* Matthew 16:24-25

Jesus also said, *"The blind will lead the blind and both will fall into the ditch."* Love is The Cross & Repentance. To surrender all and repent of sin. Not tickling ears and just telling them what they want to hear. If you are not preaching the whole Gospel with true repentance and surrendering all, then that is not love. If you love them, then you will speak the truth as you are led by The Spirit. And you are either not called or you are called, but have watered down the Gospel, which is the worst. To have an Anointing and giftings but watering down the gospel, deceiving many. You do not want to be in the ministry, if you are not called and not doing it exactly right. You are held more accountable. It will come back on you, for compromise, for self and leading people away from what is real and The Spirit. You are judged more severely. (For Study: James 3:1)

So with tears coming down my face...not knowing exactly what "Through it" meant. I said, "Lord, I don't want to have to go through it...but not my will, but Your will be done!" Just as Jesus prayed in the garden when facing the cross, He was asking if there would be any other way, but if not, "Not My Will, But Your Will Be Done." That is the prayer every Christian in their life has to pray, to accept The Cross and be a True Christian. You cannot get around surrendering to His will, to pick up Your cross and follow Him.

As the end of the year was coming, God gave me a blessing. I was 16 years old, in the 11th grade and I was praying for a car. As I prayed, I would tell the Lord what I would like. I was wanting a convertible...hey, doesn't hurt to ask. The Bible says, *"Ask whatever you will..."* So I did. The worst that can happen is God says, "No". Well, while we were traveling through West Virginia one day, we saw a car lot. We stopped to look. We saw this red mustang convertible with a black top. I still remember when I first saw it, I said, "I would take that for sure." Anyway, later on we inquired about it. We were told that someone else was getting it but if they don't come through...we could get it. The deal was, since I will be working and on work study, I would be able to make the payments. So I prayed.... "Lord, about the car...I would like it but....not my will, but your will be done."...I surrendered it. It's amazing how The Lord will see if He is first. He has to be for you to be able to handle anything, so it will not be an idol. Anyway, long story..short....They called back and said the deal fell through so, if you want it, you can get it. Are you kidding? Of course! Needless to say...We got the car!! What a blessing...fun! I would pray every time I drive and every time I would put the top down, I would pray... "Lord, may You get the glory!" Some can say, "Would God really give you a car & a convertible??"

I would say.... "Yes, He did!" Ask, whatever you will. Surrender a lot of times is the key. If something is not breaking through, maybe God is just waiting for you to surrender it, so He can give it to you the right way!! So that you can handle it, use it correctly and that He gets All the Glory.

Sure, I had some people like they always do, try & say stuff. Say I didn't pay for it etc. and a lot of other things. How immature of people. (I even paid for my insurance just in case anyone wanted to know..lol.) I always thought, everyone would be happy... that's the way I am. Happy for people when they get blessed, not envious. Especially, when it's a good person serving The Lord. This car even continues to be a blessing. Ask & receive....It is a testimony! My wife used it when we were first married and it's (my daughter) Sarah's Car Now! She got it when she was 16yrs. old like I did. She got it painted and restored, like new for Christmas, all for God's glory!

Senior Picture

I continued to seek The Lord and went on to graduate. I turned 18 and I was wondering what I was going to do, work construction with Dad, ministry or school? Mom said, "Why don't you just take a couple classes?" So I started to go to college, while also working with dad, praying for God to guide my steps-steps of faith. 2 Corinthians 5:7 says, *"For we Walk by faith, not by sight."* So be sure that if you are praying and surrendered to The Lord, He will guide your steps. And He loves faith! He will not tell you the whole plan or let you see where you are going. He wants you to Trust Him. He wants you praying and relying on Him. He has to be first; it keeps you humble and in the end, you will be so thankful and blessed you trusted Him. People will wonder how? How did this work out for you? And you will be able to say, "It's God!"

It was around this time, that my Grandma Higgs started getting me going. She knew there was a "Calling" on my life. If you knew my Grandma, she left a Godly impression. She was the real deal, a "pray-er." If she knew you, she was praying for you daily. She was the one that impressed Dad, which led to him getting SO saved. My Dad never knew a Christian so nice and real. She was all love, even if she would correct you, you thanked her for it, because you knew, it was because she loved you. She started getting me to come and teach to her 2nd grade Sunday school class and later on ministering at the nursing home. She was always in my corner. I would watch how great of a teacher she was. But I also had a problem, I hated...HATED....getting up in front of people. Many times as I felt the "Calling" of God, I would wonder how I could ever get up in front of people. I would pray for a way The Lord would help me, so I could get up in front of people. As I would teach & work with Grandma, I would pray also for a class of my own. Well, a little bit later an opening came and I took it. The Lord gave me 5th grade Sunday school class. I was loving it and I loved the kids. I would get doughnuts and play Bible basketball games. And then came an opportunity to possibly be a kids' camp counselor. As I was praying about it, they needed some counselors, and asked me. So as I was considering what to do, they started to question, not nice questions about me. "Am I mature enough?" and acting like they may not use me. Even someone close to me said, "Well, I don't know..if he can do it or not?!" It upset me. I have lived for The Lord my whole life, they know my testimony and now they are questioning me? And not some of these other kids? I was doing them a favor. So as I prayed and was about to say forget it, because they were already treating me this way. As I felt attack, one time I remember talking with Mom in the kitchen saying about attack and stuff. She would say about to persevere and to have faith etc. I said, "I know about that"..kind of annoyed. (Insert eye roll here.) When we were done talking I went in for bed and opened my Bible to read and turned right to 2 Thessalonians 1:3-5 *"We ought always to thank God for you, brothers, and rightly so, because of your faith is growing more and more, and the love all of you have for each other is increasing. Therefore, among God's churches we boast about your perseverance and faith in all the persecutions and trials you are enduring. All this is evidence that God's judgment is right and as a result you will be counted worthy for the kingdom of God for which you suffer."* Wow, what a confirmation and encouraging word of reinforcement for what I was going through. (When any time flesh people with evil intent would hear about a word or anything spiritual, they would have to try to take away, undermine or make it flesh. They would try to steal it, it's jealousy and demonic. To steal from others also, from seeing God's word for you. To say, "That's not what God meant.." on & on...So you learn you can't throw your pearls before swine. To be guarded and only share through prayer with wisdom at the right time, to the right people. So nothing can be stolen and the devil can't steal your word from God, through jealous people.) Little did I know an explosion of power was coming and it would change my life forever!

Many times God would start putting something on my heart, to open my eyes to see and wonder, it was like God was asking "Where is it?" "How come we don't see it?" It's like God would point out things that are missing. I saw it with souls, I saw that with healing and the baptism of The Holy Spirit. Then I would be praying & open to God's moving, and then see it come about. I heard them talking about last years kids' camp, how a few of the kids got filled with the Holy Spirit. I thought.. "Wow"...that is awesome, about three of them. I would then say to myself, wondering, with The Lord, "Why don't we see that more?"

So, back to the story...as I was being attacked and wondering if I should go or not? I decided after much prayer to go, saying, "So even if they get rid of me, I will just come home early." I told Mom & Dad jokingly, "Maybe see you in just a couple days." Little did I know....how big & life changing this week, with nine 9 year olds, would be!

As God would move powerfully...I saw and started to learn (and still learning) that before God would move, and as He would move and use me, that things would not go as smooth as I thought.

When breakthrough came, the waters would stir and the attack would grow. That God moves through & in spite of flesh and demonic attack. This would lead to the greatest special memories I have with God! Powerful things I will never forget and no person or demon of hades will ever take away! What God does... is forever!

Chapter 2

Precious Memories

*G*od first started putting it on my heart, to start seeing and wondering, "Where is The baptism of The Holy Spirit?" God was preparing me.

As I arrived at kids camp, (the one I almost didn't go to) I was given nine 9 year olds to take care of. I remember telling them, "I was five years old when I got baptized in The Holy Spirit and God can touch you too!" The next morning (Tuesday morning) I cannot explain it...I had never felt this way before. As I prayed, I could feel such a love, supernatural love for the kids. God put it on my heart, I could feel it. We prayed together and that night as we sat in the service, they talked about the baptism of The Holy Spirit. At the end of the service, I will never forget. They gave a call to prayer, to receive The Baptism of The Holy Spirit. One of my nine year olds turned to me and said, "I want That!!" So I said, "Let's go." I said for all of us to come down together. We got in our little group of ten and started to pray for the one that wanted filled with The Holy Spirit. And God came down! He started speaking in Tongues! And what would follow, I had never experienced in my life. One after the other, as we prayed, were filled with The Holy Spirit. I would say... "Tell them, tell them what just happened!" And the next 9yr. old would say to the other, "I just receive... I got filled with The Holy Spirit!" And there we were.... kids crying...speaking in tongues....I was on my knees praying for them...(they are so little)....with a huddle of little kids around me. Seven out of the nine, received the baptism that night, but God was not done! They kept getting more kids to come over. Little girls started getting baptized in The Holy Spirit. I knew God was moving and I looked around, I did not see the two little girls that had come, who I was also to keep an eye on. They had already left for the snack bar. I told a friend to run over and get them, "God is moving!" As we continued to pray, I was praying and staying on my knees because they are so little, I felt a hand on my shoulder. As I was praying for another kid, I peeked, it was the one little girl. Well guess who we were going to pray for next? That's right, the little girl. She got baptized in The Holy Spirit & also after that, the other little girl, was filled. There were many many kids touched & crying. You could not make this up or fake it, God was there. I remember praying for a little girl and opened my eyes because something hit my hand, it was her little tears coming off her face as God was touching her. There was another girl so touched, and just came quietly with her friend, her friend said, "She just wanted to give you a hug." So I said, "Go ahead!" With tears in her eyes, she gave me a hug. Another kid in the midst of praying, tapped me on the shoulder and said, "Hey, God spoke to me.." I said, "He did? What did He say?" "He said... "He's coming soon!"....then added with seriousness, "Sooner then you think!" Wow, that got my attention. I had another girl come up to me and say...(These are little kids...9 & 10) "God wanted me to tell you, (with tears coming down her little face)..He's really gonna use you!" The Lord moved for a couple days with more kids getting filled with The Holy Spirit and my life was changed forever!!

I remember coming home so excited but wondering a little, with all the great things that happened, why wasn't I crying? Or been teary? .....I loved it...I felt The Spirit....but didn't cry? Well, when I got home and started to tell Mom & Dad what happened, I couldn't hardly talk. I started crying....and crying ...and crying...it just hit me....and they were crying. Then I called my sister at work, telling her and she was crying. She said, "Stop you're making me cry, and I'm at work...." It was just special & Powerful!

When I got back home, God continued to move, and guess what? Some of the "religious" that didn't like who God used or how He came. They started to let the flesh get the better of them. But God continued to move.

I thought like always, "Man, people are going to want to get me, they are gonna want to put me to work. Can't they see how God is moving? They are gonna want to hear these kids' testimonies and to share what God is doing." (I was learning, it would seem to be a pattern, and I could never understand why) I would come to learn, when God would move or use me, things would not go smoother as I thought when breakthrough would come but would be worse.

One thing that is sure, when God starts to move, it starts to reveal "Truth." Who truly wants God and who does not. Who is in the flesh and who wants The Spirit. And a lot of times it's surprising both ways. Those who you think will jump in, will fight it and those you think would not want it, jump right in. And then you have a third category. Those who do not care. Who are idle, will not get hungry, in a "stupor" or a slumber and you can not get them to wake up. The lukewarm and religious are the worst. You start to find out who your true friends are. You start to see through appearances and those who are real. I started to feel the way God feels about this, *"If you are ashamed of Me and My words,...of him, The Son of Man also will be ashamed."* (Mark 8:38 & Luke 9:26.) Deny Him and He will Deny you. Ashamed of Me, I will be ashamed of you. Are you ashamed of The Gospel? Are you ashamed of God's power? Ashamed of how He moves? Some people get offended. *"Blessed are those who are not offended on account of Me."* Jesus said. Blessed are those who accept how God moves! And to whomever He chooses to move, wherever & whenever He chooses. How could people know it's right and come against it and me? How can people be so in the flesh and self and not want to glorify God?

The Bible says, *"For I am not ashamed of the gospel of Christ, for it is the power of God to salvation for everyone who believes."* Romans 1:16

When we got home, I remember someone close to me, was asking questions about being filled with The Holy Spirit. I could tell they were hungry, which is a good ingredient for receiving from God. I remember walking over to their house and started talking to them. And right there in the kitchen, Grandma & I prayed with them. They wanted to pray and got baptized in the Holy Spirit. Awesome! As the word spread, more things happened and people were receiving The gift of The Holy Spirit. I remember telling the kids in my 5th grade Sunday school class and feeling The Spirit come down. It stopped me. I said, "If you want to get prayed for....we can." Two more kids received The

Baptism. Now just to say...(Things I've learned in The school of God. Things you don't get at Bible school or can be fleshly learned, only in following The Lord. God keeps it from the wise and learned, and reveals it to babes. Arrogant, selfish people can't get it. They can't ever figure it out. Only those truly following The Lord with the right motives will God reveal His secrets to; who He can truly use. And you can't short cut the process, or you end up as you see many today, having a form but no Power! Same as salvation, if you do not have the right heart, you can be a "convert" but not "Born Again." It must be as you are drawn by The Holy Spirit to come, to truly be saved. Again, those of the flesh ministry can have "converts" but be twice as unsaved and crooked as the one who ministered to them...as Jesus said. (Matthew 23:15) You must be led by The Lord for true ministry. Those who are not truly "Called", or do not have the right heart, will never "Get It.") I don't understand how God moves. Our job is just to let Him. Make sure it's Him, in truth and if it is, don't quench or grieve Him. Don't deny The Spirit and the Power thereof. Some receive right away while others take more time. Again, it's up to The Lord. Jesus is the Baptizer in The Holy Spirit. I think sometimes The Lord wants to draw you closer, to keep you seeking Him. He uses everything to bring you closer. It was a little bit then, like the 7 sons of Sceva, people want to copy in the flesh what is done in the Spirit. (Acts 19:14) People get jealous or they want their way or whatever. I remember a child saying, "Mommy taught me how," when referring to The baptism. My friend said, "You mean prayed with you....you can't be taught it?!" But see, that's exactly what it was...taught, flesh. That's the kind of stuff that turns people off to the real. The Spirit gives you the language. Many times you can just tell by their language if it is flesh or Spirit. Sometimes if you say it, then they try to learn the right things to say, and it is still not real. People copy the right things to say but it is still not Spirit, just a flesh copy. Friend, you don't want it unless it's real!

Another time I remember, in the middle of church, I was quietly praying, "Lord, I would like someone to pray with, maybe to be filled with The Holy Spirit." I felt a touch on my shoulder. A man came over and I turned around and said, "Would you like to be prayed with to be filled with The Holy Spirit...", He said, "Yes...yes I would...." I did not know, (I found out later) at the time I was asking God to pray for someone, that man was asking a pastor, saying he wanted to be prayed with to be filled with The Holy Spirit. That pastor sent him over to me. I turned around without knowing and asked him, "Would you like to be prayed with to be filled with The Holy Spirit?"....Wow... Talk about divine appointments. As we prayed right there in the middle of the church, he lifted his hands and started praying...then he started shouting....in tongues!! What a sign that God was in the house. And that it was All God!!

I thought with all these things people would be thrilled and some are, but fleshly people can only take so much. They want the control and the glory. They start to undercut....undermine... minimize...etc. So after a while, I was surprised by the response & lack of response. Also, resulting in a lack of opportunities. I would see the church get either the outward appearances which is wrong or the newly converted which is OK for a testimony, but not to be examples or leaders in the church yet. (1 Timothy 3:6) Also, they would get people that don't live holy, and other things that are against what the Word of God says. It is for their sake and the church's, to do it according to what the Word of God says. They say you can't judge. Yes, there is wrong judging, but there are times you have to test and judge things or it is anything goes. That is why false teachers and false brothers etc. have been allowed to spread because of the false teaching. They used the wrong false teaching way about "judging." The wrong judging is actually not allowing people to get right, they don't tell them it's wrong. We just need to go by the guidelines of the Bible. The Bible says to test everything. These same people then turn around and say you are wrong & judging, when in fact that is just what they did...judge me and said I am wrong. So...either you can say things are wrong or everyone has to let everything go and be quiet. That is so wrong. You can just judge the ones living right all day and reject them, but someone in sin, you can't? That is a twist....The "judgment twist." That gets the fake & gets rid of the real. That my friend is why there is a form of godliness and "no- power" churches. (For Study: 1 Corinthians 5:11-13, 1 Corinthians 6:9-10)

After a while people who loved you, (because of the twist & lying by the flesh) & ones that got a touch from God...with you.... end up hating you and blaming you. But people know what is right and wrong. Everyone has a choice and everyone really knows it too, but some think it is easier to go with sin, the wrong and jus- tify it. But really, in the end, it kills. Go with the cross first, and stay living right and standing for what's right. It might be hard at first, but I couldn't live with myself and how wimpy to know and choose the wrong, just so that you don't get any flack or try to fit in. What is tough and cool, is doing what's right no matter what.

By God's grace, never bow. I would rather die, then bow to the wicked and sin. Listen, don't let the devil steal, through jealous people, your true friends & your miracles from God!!

All that it takes is one person to be upset when someone is requesting to get you to minister and people give in. They want no one upset but, you have to fight and get what is right or all you have is fake and watered down. Yeah it looks good and is accepted by everyone but is nothing spiritually. It deceives away from the real. I want the real things of God.

The next year, at kids camp, I saw one of the most powerful things I have ever seen. A little girl's powerful touch. As the next year's camp was again powerful. I wondered after a service one night, where this little girl close to me, was at? Little did I know, what amazing thing, I was about to see. As I walked over to where the girls were, most had left to go to the snack bar, but around the altar, there she was, lying on the ground, shaking and crying out to God. She was powerfully hit with intercession that only God can do. Only God could do this through someone who was yielded to Him. She would cry out... "No...Jesus....No!!" And would push away with her hands....as she shook,....she would again, cry out.... "No....Jesus...No!!!" (I can't hardly write this as I cry) That went on for awhile, she would then sit up and look at me, then be back on the ground shaking & crying. I would just watch and pray, as this was going on. So amazed. No way this could be faked, an 11yr. old little child. She then got up and came over and sat down beside me on the front pew. I said, "What is going on?" (I was dying to know what God is doing, what is He saying?) She said, "Well, I was praying for my family..." She put her head down..... and did a front flip off the pew....and was back down with God all over her, crying and shaking, hit by the power of God. I was just amazed and reverent, I could not believe what God was doing. I could see God moving so powerfully right before my eyes. She got up again, I was asking her, "What is God saying?" She said, "I was praying for my family...." (For salvation)..... Then I prayed for her and I asked her to pray for me because I wanted whatever she had. As she prayed for me...She fell back again...and I caught her in my arms and let her down easy. She was interceding again. Just let God do whatever.... He wants to do! I just watched and prayed in amazement. She then after all this interceding, started to laugh, be relieved and refreshed by God. Now, right here I want to say something. Yes, 100% test and be cautious with everything. BUT, if it is GOD....don't touch it!! Because then you are messing with God and will be held accountable if You speak against The Holy Spirit moving. To blaspheme The Holy Spirit is the only sin you cannot be forgiven of. Matthew 12:31 says, *"Therefore I say to you, every sin and blasphemy will be forgiven men, but the blasphemy against The Spirit will not be forgiven men."* This was not the end of the story. Flesh people get bent all out of shape right here...my question is why? Ever read the Bible? Ever see the miracles Jesus did? How the fake church would respond? Be offended at The Lord? Be careful where you fall when God is moving, what group are you in? Are you trying to figure out why? Rather then, God knows "Why?". Just as long as it's God... and there are signs and wonders that show it's Him... is "Why?" sometimes. So the rest of the story.... It actually had a powerful effect later... it broke through miracles, by The Spirit, and being used in intercession by an 11yr.old. I would ask, "What was that?",... She said, well, she was praying for her family, and she didn't really know what happened, or that anyone could see her having all this. She was just starting to intercede and pray, God just took over. She would shake, it didn't hurt or wasn't scary but like working, (intercession) it is a good work you want and never want to leave. She said when she would say "No....Jesus....No!!" and push away with her hands, she said, as she was praying for her family to get saved, the devil would come and tell her... "stop praying, they are never going to get saved...." That's when she would cry out and say.... "No....Jesus...NO!!" As if to say, "Jesus, you have to save them....." Wow....So powerful....that is intercession right there..... by The Holy Spirit, praying for them to be saved. So, as that went on and when it was over, she said it was like God's face came into hers and she was laughing, it was like a relief after all the intercession. It was broke through. God was going to save her family. Needless to say....are you ready? A few months later, her relative got saved. This powerful intercession was showing true. So powerful. Be sure though, the devil and jealous church do not like it. It is our responsibility, (a lot do not realize this) you have to guard what God gives you. You have to do your part, and stay doing your part, if you want to see it <u>all</u> come to fruition. Meaning if you give up on God's word or get into sin, listen to the devil and evil jealous people, it can stop God's word from being completed in your life. And then actually turn and destroy you. You can have a "Calling" or a word, but if you don't stay in God's will, pay the price or whatever, be trusted, you will forfeit that special thing in your life. Like Samson, he would have never been captured, if he stayed faithful doing his part. And everyone knew it was God and powerfully coming about by miracles, already proven. The devil will say to the one who had the word, "See, it's not coming about," etc.. Don't believe or listen to them! If you do, it can lead you into sin and destroys what God has spoken and that is what it did. But, people are held accountable, so are the ones who know what God says and then listens to the devil and gives it up.

As we shared the powerful testimony, people would try consistently to undermine & give credit everywhere but where it belongs, giving God glory. People try to say things like, "You take all the attention" etc; which are all lies from a greedy heart. Anything to steal & distract from what God is doing. Make up false arguments, to steal from who God is using and for people to not listen to that, but to them. There would be people putting pressure on anyone, to not be around. Then try to blame me why they're not around. But people know the truth if they want it and have a choice. Sadly sometimes they go with the easy way, with what's wrong. So they don't look "bad" instead of taking care of the sin. It's not good enough just to know it is wrong and who is wrong. Eli (in the Bible) knew, but lost everything because he didn't take care of it. Don't say, "I can't do anything" or "I can't make them", you can take stands for correction. As scripture says, then and only then, when they bear fruit in keeping with repentance, can it be made right. Not just words, it has to be walked out. I love people, even the wicked enough, to not let them continue to destroy themselves and others and that they have a chance to get right.

There have been times and different scenarios, I would be confronted by ones trying to deceive and just put up a front, they knew they were lying, causing problems and I knew they were lying but they were still trying to play the game and put up a front. I would then agree to just move on but they would said "No".

Then, pretending to be "great Christians" would say I was the one not wanting to work it out. There are people out there like that, That is a heart of deception and some people believe the ones causing dissension. Even ones that know they are wrong, still sometimes go with them because they didn't want to appear as unforgiving and fear retribution. That's how they get control, no matter how much they falsely accuse, you must deal with it until it is stopped. If they never repent, then you have to stay standing forever. You can not allow this to go on, for their sake, yours and everyone else's. Dissension has to be stopped. Romans 16:17 *"Now I beseech you, brethren, mark them which cause divisions and offenses contrary to the doctrine which ye have learned; and avoid them."* The Bible says how to deal with sin, dissension and how to deal with people who say they are Christian but are living in sin. Have Nothing To Do With Them. (1 Corinthians 5:9-11 & Matthew 18:15-17) They should feel ashamed and repent but if not, you cannot allow it to spread, cause more damage and take everyone captive because no one will confront it. It leads people astray, keeps them captive and ruins lives. No, you have to stand until it is corrected and or it is completely stopped. It will not continue one way or the other. And people know but do not want any trouble, will compromise to be around them, against what scripture says, so it spreads. It will hurt you and many other people. Destroying families, friendships, ministry and on & on. I say, guard, protect and stand the right way, no matter what.

Everyone wants "Called", but the Bible specifically says, *"And no man takes this honor upon himself but he that is Called of God..."* Hebrews 5:4. People want the honor, they want the prestige but for the real there is always a price first. People try to take the honor upon themselves and this is what causes a mess. It tries to take away from the real and deceives because there is no persecution and there is no cross...it's all flesh. So they can be promoted & promote themselves quickly & others like them and it's not spirit no matter how hard they try or what people say. It's up to God. So they have a form of Godliness but no power, from such turn away. They are self, no matter how humble they appear. There should be signs of "Calling" if you're truly "Called." Signs, not of people but undeniable signs, miracles from God. You have to want the truth & have the right heart. You truly know if you are honest, willing to accept the cross and truth, no matter what. We have too many self... "Called" or people "Called" and there is no Anointing, just performance, that people confuse as Anointing. There is No True Power, conviction of The Holy Spirit or signs & wonders that follow those who believe. Now I believe everyone can be used and should be used. People can have gifts of The Spirit. (9 Spiritual Gifts ...1 Corinthians 12: 4-11 *"There are diversities of gifts, but the same Spirit. There are differences of ministries, but the same Lord. And there are diversities of activities, but it is the same God who works all in all. But the manifestation of The Spirit is given to each one for the profit of all; for to one is given the word of wisdom through The Spirit, to another the word of knowledge through the same Spirit, to another faith by the same Spirit, to another gifts of healings by the same Spirit, to another the working of miracles, to another prophecy, to another discerning of spirits, to another different kinds of tongues, to another the interpretation of tongues. But one and the same Spirit works all these things, distributing to each one individually as He wills."*) But this is different from The

"Called" leaders of the church. Things must be in order for God to move. The Bible says in Ephesians 4:11, *"And He gave some to be apostles, some prophets, some evangelists, and some pastors and teachers, for equipping of the saints for the work of ministry..."* He gave "some" not all. Flesh, the rebellious and the like, want to come in and not have to listen to their "Godly Authority" which really is not listening to God. Now yes, test everything and make sure nothing is off but, if it's truth & you reject God's "Called", it's not man you're rejecting but God! The Bible says, *"For the time will come when they will not endure sound doctrine, but according to their own desires, because they have itching ears, they will heap up for themselves teachers; and they will turn their ears away from the truth...."* 1 Tim. 4:3-4. The church & people will instead of accepting the Truth & The "Called", will get the non-"Called"or try & scare, force, the ones "Called", to tickle their ears and water down the Gospel. Then after a time of feeding on tickled ears, when the real message comes & the real power comes, the Cross is preached and repentance from sin is preached....people can't take it. They get offended. They don't want to hear it... it's killing their flesh. Anything flesh is fine, the non-"Called" or the watered down appearances, but if the real shows up, they will get rid of them. They will falsely accuse and say, "unloving", "condemning", "judgmental", "legalistic" on & on. Anything to keep you from saying about sin. Don't get caught up in the appearance "acts." Make sure there is the real; has to be power & holiness flowing together. Anything else is just an act. I want the church to have discernment so that people are not deceived into perishing & being sickly. Jesus warned of false teachers, false prophets & false doctrines. That the Blind lead the blind and both will fall into the ditch. So be warned and we should warn about it. It's not wrong to check & be cautious, it's wrong not to. It's a must! So we do not get into goofy things. That's what turns honest people off and the lost that would truly come to The Lord. It keeps them from salvation. Jesus said, *"But woe to you, scribes and Pharisees, hypocrites! For you shut up the kingdom of heaven against men, for you neither go in yourselves, nor do you allow those who are entering to go in."* Matthew 23:13. This in the church... ministers, people, keeping others from true repentance. I've seen it! Saying they are "OK" and will keep people from getting the sin out, that they want to be free from. They keep them from repentance. People, pastors not even giving altar calls for repentance & salvation. (William Booth, founder of The Salvation Army said, "I consider that the chief dangers which confront the coming century will be religion without the Holy Ghost, Christianity without Christ, forgiveness without repentance, salvation without regeneration, politics without God, and heaven without hell.")

I've seen where we've had kids want to come to church, from our youth outreach. They would get up and wait outside by themselves for the church van to pick them up. The "church" people would not get them. They were offended. They didn't like the way they looked or etc. for whatever reason. It's wrong and sin. I began to see that it's not the kids that are rebellious, but it's some of the church. They are keeping those who would come, from coming, because they want to "play" church. When things are religious, the real and those who want the real, will not be accepted. The fake do not want the real to come, it's too convicting to their false living. SO in a lot of cases, it's not you.... the reason why sometimes the church is a turn off, it's not because your bad....but because you want the real and they are fake. It's not The Lord that would make you feel that way, it's the fake hypocrites. Jesus loves you and wants you to come. But go where He is wanted, where it's The Spirit, fresh & real. I learned, as I saw these kids come to The Lord, night after night every Friday, that they want the real and will respond when it's real. And it's a lot of the church that really don't want repentance, true repentance. It was around this time that The Lord would teach me a lesson I will never forget. It was when the pastor was gone and I was in charge of the service. I was to preach in the morning and to play a video at night. So during the morning, I preached and gave an altar call. Some responded to get right with The Lord. One specifically, was a young 10yr old girl who responded. I saw her hand and I had everyone pray with me. Inside though, when I saw her hand, I thought to myself, she probably doesn't know really what's she's doing. I prayed and led everyone to pray with me. Anyway that night, as I started the video, and sat down as the church watched the film...God started to deal with me. He brought that little girl to my mind and God said, *"Who do you think you are, thinking that, that little girl did not really want me?"* I started to cry, and I repented before The Lord, asking for Him to give me another chance. Who am I? I of all people that got saved when I was 4 yrs. old and filled with The Holy Spirit when I was 5. I did give the altar call but... I took it lightly. You see, that little girl would get up on Sundays, all by herself, as Her parents did not go to church. She got ready, all alone and would wait outside by herself for the van. You never know when she will be back or with anyone, if you will have another chance. If they will have another chance to be able to get right with God. DO not miss one opportunity! Well, after the video was over and I had been dealt with by God. After praying for God to give me another chance, I got up to finish the service and who do you think I saw in the back? Yep, that little girl. I had another chance! I told the church how God had just dealt with me, that I took it lightly. I repented! I told that girl I am sorry and everyone about taking it lightly. So I gave the altar call, and God moved! The altar was filled with people coming to repent and make things right with God! God was there, His presence! God had given me another chance, and may we never... ever take it lightly for someone to have a chance to be Saved. To know and give their life to The Lord!! God will show up when we repent! Repentance is an attractor to God's presence. To humble ourselves and pray. To seek His face and TURN from our wicked ways. Then He will hear from heaven, forgive our sin and heal our land! (2 Chr. 7:14) (Pray & repent right now. Ask Him to forgive & He will. So that times of refreshing may come from the presence of The Lord; Repent & feel His refreshing Presence. (Acts 3:19)(Do it now, if you need to.) People grieve The Spirit, so not to offend, to make sure no one is offended...so grieve The Holy Spirit? No, then no ministry happens if you do not let Him move and let God worry about the few that might be upset. It's God they are upset with, and will have to give an account for it. Don't you be in that & keep people from being ministered to, because you were scared of a "few." Be scared not to let God move. They were upset with Jesus, they will be upset with you. Aren't you glad He didn't let anyone stop Him from touching you? Go & do likewise. If you don't, it's not true ministry. I know later on, that is why we would see powerful miracles...healings...and unusual miracles etc. Because we let God have His way but we were also rejected by the religious and a lot of the area because of it. Even if people liked it, they would be too scared to be a part. Then they turn around and are always the ones saying they never get fed and on & on. So they stay in their dry, dead church. I would be scared not to be a part of what is right. Scared to reject the real, to stay with the half-hearted? No, and stop complaining, if you will not leave the clique, social club to go to the real, whether it be big or a small group. Only matters if it's Jesus! I've seen both, big & beautiful but sickening, & small & rough but amazing and God moving! Remember, God chose a stable to be born in & only a few that listened, got to be there! And there was only a few on Noah's boat. Be careful of the "Majority" because the "Many" are on the road that leads to destruction but narrow & hard the road that leads to life and few will be that find it. (Matthew 7:14) Count me with the few. The superficial make me sick and makes The Lord sick too. That's why many are turned off to the church today. They have lost being real. They have lost the point. You end up with a form and fake. No true repentance, just people using the church for their own selfish reasons. And they turn off people that would truly get saved, as well as those who are real. They attack & reject them. Just a bunch of fake nothing, flesh.... sin. Jesus said, *"I wish you were cold or hot. So then because you are lukewarm, and neither cold nor hot, I will vomit you out of My mouth."* Revelation 3:15-16. Makes The Lord sick.

When you're on the cross, in God's will, it's like it's "OK" for people to reject you. Not get you etc...but if you're in the flesh...not "Called" or not living right, a new convert, they can't say "No." When the Bible says the complete opposite. **1 Timothy**

3:1-5 (Qualifications of Overseers) " *This is a faithful saying: If a man desires the position of a bishop, he desires a good work. A bishop then must be blameless, the husband of one wife, temperate, sober-minded, of good behavior, hospitable, able to teach; not given to wine, not violent, not greedy for money, but gentle, not quarrelsome, not covetous; one who rules his own house well, having his children in submission with all reverence (for if a man does not know how to rule his own house, how will he take care of the church of God?);* " & **Titus 1:5-9 (Qualified Elders)** "*For this reason I left you in Crete, that you should set in order the things that are lacking, and appoint elders in every city as I commanded you— if a man is blameless, the husband of one wife, having faithful children not accused of dissipation or insubordination. For a bishop must be blameless, as a steward of God, not self-willed, not quick-tempered, not given to wine, not violent, not greedy for money, but hospitable, a lover of what is good, sober-minded, just, holy, self-controlled, holding fast the faithful word as he has been taught, that he may be able, by sound doctrine, both to exhort and convict those who contradict.* " *(For study: Proverbs 23:31-32, Proverbs 20:1)*

If you want to have special memories & see powerful things in God and in your life, it will come only through obedience, a price, and a complete surrender. It will go against the flow, but it is well worth it & no other way around it; If you want to be close to God, be used & see His power!

Chapter 3

Lessons From God

(The Price and Seriousness Intensifies)

*A*s I felt "Called", I would wonder, how I would ever be able to get up in front of people....I hated it. I would get about sick if I had to do anything up in front of people. So I would pray, "Lord, give me a way that I would be able to get up in front of people... help me to be able to minister. Give me an easier way, to get used to it." Well, little did I know the complete unorthodox way that God would use. Such a blessing & a help to me. (As God's power and use of me increased, so did the price, attack & seriousness intensify.) And amazing powerful Words from God that would confirm His "Call"on my life.

At the time I was 19 yrs old, I got voted on to be Youth Group President. It started off by us wanting to go early and pray before the service, for God to move & have His way. Well, after a little time when everyone else stopped going early to pray...I still felt a drawing...I was hungry.....God was drawing me closer, and it's a promise, *"Draw near to God & He will Draw near to you."* If you do your part, God will show up...and one day He did! As I was just seeking Him, I remember so clearly. I was going to have to get up and do prayer requests & pray, in front of the Youth group. Well, as I got up and took requests...and started to pray.... all the sudden by surprise...I felt The Spirit of God come down... and my hands started to shake...I really felt The Lord. I prayed and said about feeling God. If you go after Him....be sure, one day...He will show up!

Everything just made me more hungry. As I went after God there was a move of opposition that started to try and move me out of my role. (By the way....these are things you learn by God, when you are "Called" by God. You can only learn in the school of God....that you can't get in Bible school.)

What the devil meant for evil, God used to open a new door of ministry and add a blessing to me. What caused me to move on, was actually a move up. A person who was causing problems, instead of taking care of it, they appeased it. Some of the leaders gave the one who was lying, my position of prayer. So at the same time, God opened the door for me to move on and these same ones that didn't take care of it...well, it actually came back to affect them directly. (They came back later and apologized to me, but people still didn't take care of it. It's not good enough to know...but the problem must be removed & stopped; as scripture tells us. The Bible is clear on how to deal with sin and someone causing division. Too many times rather then take care of it, people appease it and the good one is hurt along with other people. While the one causing it is not corrected. They continue to hurt others & themselves. Correct it, for their sake and everyone else's. DO what the Bible says, take care of it until it does not continue, however long that takes. On a side note, sadly this is another thing you never hear about or rarely see put into action. The good ones are run off while they keep the ones causing the problem.)

So while all this was going on at the same time, a trip I will never forget, was when our youth group went to a Christian concert. I liked the group, but as I sat there seeing a lot of performance, God was working on me and about to answer my prayer and to give me a way to be able to get up in front of people. I was starting to get more annoyed at "performance" rather than seeing The moving of The Spirit. I don't want a concert, a show. We need real ministry, the Power of God to touch lives. See, once you're truly touched by the Spirit and your eyes are opened...once you taste the Real thing, nothing else...nothing less will satisfy! I said, "Lord, I promise...If you ever give me anything like this...to play an instrument or worship, to be up in front of people, I promise...I will do it ALL unto You!!" Four weeks later, I was asked to start a worship team and within four more weeks of picking up the guitar...(I could not play)....within four weeks....I was up playing my guitar, leading the worship, playing four songs. It was a miracle! And a prayer I still pray, every time I pick up a guitar....I pray, "Lord, ALL unto YOU!" I have kept my promise and He answered my prayer with giving me something to help me get up in front of people to minister. Now yes, I started with not hardly looking out (lol) and just focusing on Him and I would say to help me, "No matter how it sounds...it's all unto You Lord!" It's for The Lord.....**I only & always play for an audience of ONE!**

I only & always play for an audience of One!

At first, my Dad wasn't sure about me playing it around him because we are an athletic family, sports, etc. and wanted it all unto The Lord. But it ended up, when he saw it ALL unto The Lord, I would worship in my parents' bedroom until they fell asleep...they loved it! What a difference true worship makes, when it's done right and you can be manly, like David who killed Goliath & worshiped on his harp; a Psalmist. There's also a higher worship that goes beyond words, singing and songs. There are spiritual songs. (For Study: Psalms 150, John 4:23-34, Matthew 15:8, Ephesians 5:19)

Side Note: Gifts & Talents; Spiritual & Physically. Whatever gifts or talents you have, do all for God's glory. Be led by The Spirit and surrendered to Him. So that it will be a blessing to you and a return for what God has deposited in you, for His kingdom.

So it will not be taken from you, a curse to you but more added to you. (For Study: Matthew 25:14-30, 1 Corinthians10:31, 1 Peter 5:6)

Doors started to open and I have always been the kind that I don't want it, unless I know it's God. I do not want to promote myself. It has to be God to open The door and His timing or I don't want it. Others that, "Do & Go", on their own, it's for self and not GOD! And many today are taught that's how it's done. That's the way the not "Called" teach it. Let God open the way....then it's for His Glory & of The Spirit-true ministry! Another trip that was life changing, was when I first saw videos of the Brownsville revival baptisms and testimonies. Right away, when I saw them so touched, the people who were sharing testimonies,...I did not even wonder if this was God, I knew it was and in my heart I said... "I want that!" The church ended up taking a trip to the revival and after long debate whether to go or not, I did. Waited in line all day, seeking The Lord. The service was awesome and I went to get prayed for at the end and I had never felt anything like that before. I could feel The Spirit of God jumping around inside me so powerfully. I felt intercession on the way home, it was a great push in prayer that I had for a long time after. There was attack and a lot more to this story but my life was power-fully touched and changed. Once you taste of the Spirit, for real... nothing else will satisfy. I would just get more and more hungry for God. (Which is a good sign of a healthy Christian.... You are hungry for the things of God. If you do not have a good appetite, then something is wrong, and you may be sick, spiritually.)

(These are things you learn, when you are "Called" by God and pass the tests. Those that fail, do not get it. They do not learn and cannot be led by the Spirit. Fail the tests and all you are in, is flesh. And God knows the difference and the heart. Those that will not pass the tests and those that are willing to be taught and can grow in use.) (For Study: 1 Corinthians 2:13-14, 1 Corinthians 1:18-31)

Around this time as God was moving, (Moving with the worship and people getting filled with The Holy Spirit, signs & wonders) that attack would increase. People started to twist and make up lies, which is the enemy's favorite tactic. To minimize, to undercut, to give a wrong slant on the innocent party and to protect & give control to the wrong party. To feel sympathetic to the ones lying instead of the one actually innocent. So the selfish can get control, tear others down & build themselves up. So attack grew and people would twist & put pressure on everyone around me. If you are scared of the pressure, scared to look bad, scared to upset the liars and want your own way, which they will help you & still say it's God, then you give in. Rather than stand, many give in and don't stand for what's right. It's easier to give in or play dumb, but God knows. The right thing to do is stand. People then get bound up by the false & can't get out because they are bound by the lies. They bind you to have to be around "wolves", otherwise you are not "loving" or you are "condemning" or "unforgiving". When it's not you, it's them that need to repent! Repent and walk it out, not just tell others to get over it & the "wolves" stay free to continue to cause problems. Have nothing to do with them is what the Bible says! God's people need to live by what the Bible says, for the "wolves'" sake to have a chance to get right & to protect yourself & everyone else. Remember you deserve what you tolerate. If you let "wolves" around your family, don't wonder why your kids are getting devoured. (For Study: Matthew 7:15-20)

Bad company corrupts good morals. Don't be caught in the trap to risk yourself to "reach out." If it's God, He will give you a safe way to reach out.

As God's fire and attack grew, I was needing a Word from The Lord. So we set out on a trip to seek The Lord & to hear from Him. We were all praying and asking God to touch and to speak to me. To confirm what is going on and bring clarity. And boy was God going to speak! Little did we know one of the most powerful Life Words I would ever have...would come.

Our trip started, that we would travel and stop at our Pastor friend's house & church in South Carolina. Pastor Owen, a trusted man of God, was one of the few we trusted. Then we also planned to continue on to The Brownsville Revival. We stopped to talk to Pastor Owen and go to the revival service he was having. So as we talked, we still could not get clarity. Then at the service that night of an evangelist, that did not know us at all, during the service had a Word from The Lord...2/1/98....*He said, "There is someone here or a few people, that the Lord has a Word for with a* "......, ..." He used a term I've never heard before and then went on to say, *"You struggle with identity, but you do have an identity. You find relief for a time, in the service, but afterwards you still have it. It's gone on for a long time....."* I was praying about it. Mom & Dad were thinking it was for me and Pastor Owen also pondered the word. But, I didn't know. I thought I don't know if it's for me or not. I don't know about identity or not? But I do feel that All the lies did affect me. So, I wondered about it but still didn't know. After that, three days later we made it to Florida, to visit the revival that was going on there. I talked with a Pastor beforehand, trying to explain what I was going through but he didn't seem to understand what I was saying. He was nice but I could not get the answers I was looking for. So before the service that night, we were all praying. I was asking God to speak to me. I needed a word from Him that I knew was from Him. Little did I know that God and only God could do and speak in a way that He was going to. It was one of the most powerful words I would ever receive. As we were in the service, the worship was about over and the Youth Pastor, Pastor Crisco ... interrupted Pastor Kilpatrick and said, "Excuse me Pastor, I have a Word.... I have a Word for *"Someone or a few people who The Lord has a word for with a "......., ..."* Used the exact same term I had never heard of before. Needless to say, it got our attention....we knew it was God! Mom, right away sat down and started writing the word..... Here is the full word...... 2/4 /98... *"You are climbing a mountain but unable to reach the plateau, and when it is in sight, you lose your footing and drop back down to despair and even to the point of death. Then if that was not bad enough, the flood waters come in, when you are down and as you are about to go under, The Lord pulls your head above the waters. You have tried many times and just before you reach the top you fall again. All your life trying to reach the pinnacle of your dreams. This flood of water you interpret as the devil coming in. You try to figure it out and understand it. You have talked to people about this...You need to relax. The Flood is really God helping to push you up to the top of your pinnacle, the point you keep trying to reach. In fact it is salt water because you have wounds that you have gotten from your whole life, all over your whole body and the salt water is to heal up those wounds....* (As mom was already writing this down, he said....) *You'll need to write down this vision.*"

It was an unbelievable word of God. Undeniable for me, confirmed! This is the promise God gave me...and me and my Grandma painted this word and is the picture, representation of our cover of this book.... "I Promise" From God.

"I Promise"

This painting hangs in my house as a reminder of God's promise to me.

Now, I want to say right here, when you have special things from God, be careful. Guard them, protect them....keep it safe. "People" when they would hear the Word, started to twist and would try to use it against me. Jealousy is very powerful...it caused Cain to kill Abel...it caused the brothers of Joseph to throw him in a pit & sell him into slavery. When people do things wrong &

you do it the right way...they should get it right...not attack the one doing it right. Anyhow, instead of honor from God & for paying a price for God's glory, it's made to mock. Especially when it's a God thing. I would learn that this would be a pattern. So I learned I had to be careful in sharing the things of God. People try and steal the Words. (There are so many fake copies, don't be a copy, be an original. So many fake copies of me & things in my life. Get your own life, in God.) As the devil does, he comes to steal, kill and to destroy, everything God does. Scripture says, *"Do not give what is holy to the dogs; nor cast your pearls before swine, lest they trample them under their feet, and turn and tear you to pieces."* Matthew 7:6. <u>The devil is always in the "ifs", never in the answers.</u> Just questions, wonder and doubt. The forked tongue works, causing & planting seeds of suspicion, evil & strife. One against another. James 3:14-16 says, *" But if you have bitter envy and self-seeking in your hearts, do not boast and lie against the truth. This wisdom does not descend from above, but is earthly, sensual, demonic. For where envy and self seeking exist, confusion and every evil thing are there."* The Bible says, *"Now I urge you, brethren, note those who cause divisions and offenses, contrary to the doctrine which you learned, and avoid them."* Romans 16:17. And avoid them!! Other places The Bible says, "Have nothing to do with them", "With such people do not even eat!" We get in trouble and wickedness spreads when we do not stand and do what God's Word says to do. The righteous are persecuted, more people are hurt and led astray. DO what God says to do. I got attacked for it, but it is the only way for what's right to be protected and a chance for the wicked to get right. Compromise makes it worse and protects evil, to do more evil. It is not love to let people continue to do evil; to stand is love.

So before leaving for my first year away from home, to go to Southeastern Bible school, I was armed with the word of The Lord I received from our trip at Pastor Owen's and Brownsville Revival. I was feeling led to go away now to school. I stopped at a church in West Virginia. The Pastor Gave a powerful Word, and a sign to me. I had never seen this before. The Pastor, while ministering felt led by The Lord, that God wanted to place a mantle on me. (This is a Pastor that would not just do this, and had never done that before or since. In the middle of the service, he came down, took his jacket off, and placed it on me. God was giving me a mantle. It was special and powerful. Something I needed before leaving for Southeastern. And later on I would see how it would come into play again.)

(Side note: It has always been weird to see that when people have a word for me or seen God do amazing things in my life, instead of getting me, "they" many times, would get anybody but me. See it's easier to get the flesh than the real and so they go close but not the cross, not the Spirit. Because everyone will not like The Spirit or accept The Spirit like they do the flesh. The flesh always tries to get you to come off the cross. They get a fake copy and they know better; seen this about a "million" times. *Even up to this point, after all these years & many books sold, I had not been asked to share my testimony; perhaps, if God wills, that will change. Part of the problem today is getting the flesh & "accepted" rather then what is proven, solid, real & will help people's lives.* Also, a warning: don't copy the signs God gave to me. When it's God, He will speak continually new & fresh, don't be a fake copy. Get your own real words and signs from God!)

As I felt led to go to Southeastern, I would get into surfing and basketball, but it was hard to leave my nieces & nephews, family and my friends. Little did I know that when I was gone, I was left unprotected and the undercutting current against me would grow & take a lot of "those close to me" away. Only listening to lies and the people I know that did not have their best interest at heart. How can you blame me, when you are not listening to me but them....duh?! I saw how God feels when people don't listen to Him or His Word and then that's the first one they start blaming (Him) when things don't work out. It wasn't God, it was you choosing your own way. God tried to warn you and tell you a different way but you didn't listen, but He still loves you. Like many prodigals, it's time to come home. You have to do your part & He will forgive. This evil current starts slyly... slowly...like a python...slowly constricting....for selfish gain. We ended up moving on.

So as we moved on, at the end of the school year, we went to another church. The very first service we attended there, a man who did not know me at all was ministering. When I went forward to get prayed for, as they wanted to pray for all the college kids and again, it was at a new church: they had a new person ministering. He gave me a Word, had no idea who I was and said as he prayed for me, *"You've kept yourself pure, & you need to take the Mantle God has already given you!"* Wow!! He was touched, he later said to my family, a year or so later, that giving that word to me was a Highlight of his ministry. He did not know me, but said about being pure and also about the mantle, that I was just given a year before. Now, I was making decisions feeling led to go to Brownsville for the school of ministry. I was so thankful for God confirming my steps and speaking. I would not want it any other way. When you pay a price and stay in God's will, then He will speak and confirm things to you in special ways. This is not so if you are on your own, your own way, there is no "special"... there is no "divine." I want, in the steps of this life, God's divine hand and signs in my life. And with all these things, promises and when God speaks to you, when He uses you, we must be trusted. We must do our part and not compromise or give up, if we want to keep the promises and if we want to see them come about; if we want to continue to be used and see God's divine. Luke 12:48 *"For everyone to whom much is given, from him much will be required; and to whom much has been committed, of him they will ask the more."*

(Pray right now, for God's divine to be in your life, surrender your ways & give Him the OK to do whatever He wants to do with your life. Be trusted & see His miraculous, divine hand & signs in your life....In Jesus Name! Amen.)

Chapter 4

Accusations Through Preparations

With attack, comes The Divine intervention. Many times before attack or before a great task in the Bible, God would give a word to people that would sustain them through the attack. It would give them the courage and strength to do what God was asking them to do because God knew that they would need it. It is the same today. Like how it was with Moses. God Called him and showed him powerful signs.. because of the big task ahead. Just like before Jesus' testing in the wilderness, God spoke at His baptism...Remember? God spoke from Heaven saying, *"This is My beloved Son with whom I Am well pleased!"* and then He was immediately led by the Spirit to be tempted by the devil. And the first thing the devil said was,"If, you are the Son of God......" trying to get Him to doubt God's Word over Him, what God just spoke and get Him in the flesh. The devil wanted Jesus to go in the flesh and use His power in the flesh, to break His fast; to give Jesus a way around the Cross, not to have to suffer but to get it in the flesh. It's easier and faster. But It's flesh, sin and not Spirit. He chose to suffer and not get all the kingdoms of the Earth given to Him...the flesh way. But Jesus said, *"It is written,*

'Man, shall not live by bread alone, but by every word that pro-ceeds from the mouth of God." Jesus didn't give into flesh or twisted excuses of God's word, to get Him into the flesh but used God's Word in context to keep Him surrendered to God's will, and not to put God to the test. He was able to stay obedient and came out of the desert, having passed the tests, in the Power of God. Then, and only then, was He ready for ministry and had The Spirit of God and power. Luke 4:14 says, *"Then Jesus returned in the power of The Spirit to Galilee, and news of Him went out through all the surrounding region."* Now if that's how it was for Jesus, how much more so for us? Many, sadly who are Called, either avoid the desert testing first and just run into ministry out of God's will and timing or they fail the tests in the desert. Either way, they come out with no power. Just flesh ministry. Forms of godliness and no power. (For Study: 2 Timothy 3:5, 1 Corinthians 1:17) And many run into ministry who are not even "Called." So no matter how "nice" it seems or how many people like it, in the end you're killing people off by a powerless gospel. Because it's deceiving them away from the truth, anointed of God, giving them a way around obedience and fighting against those who truly are carrying the Cross. You end up fighting against the power and real ministry. You fight against the Spirit because you never had the flesh burnt out of you, gold refined in the fire because you did not surrender completely to God. And hence, creating a lot of the problems of the church today and of the blind leading the blind. And of the true ministers, who are for God's glory, being persecuted and rejected. The flesh likes that, how it is, (flesh & self glorifying) those truly "Called" can't stand the fake deceiving flesh. They truly want to see people saved and God to get the

glory and not a selfish deceiving man. Those truly "Called" will have that wilderness and refining fire first... then come out in holiness, the power of God and for God's glory. Revelation 3:18 says, *"I counsel you to buy from Me gold refined in the fire..."* Another powerful verse is I Corinthians 2:4-5 that says, *"And my speech and my preaching were not with persuasive words of human wisdom, but in a demonstration of The Spirit and of Power, that your faith should not be in the wisdom of men but in The Power of God."* And as scripture also says, *"That the kingdom of God is not a matter of talk but of power."* 1 Corinthians 4:20. What separates everything, from the flesh and of every false religion in the world is... The power of God! Proof is in the Power. No power, no calling... Signs and wonders will follow those who believe and God will confirm His word (and "Calling") through the accompanying signs.

And it is the same for us today. The devil will tempt, especially those "Called" to get it "Now." Instead of waiting on The Lord and His timing but are tested & hearing a voice saying... "Don't suffer, that is stupid...look over there, they are getting ministry "now"...they are liked by everyone....why are you suffering and no one sees? No one cares, it's All for nothing...." WRONG! That is a lie. Theirs is in the flesh and is all for nothing. They have nothing divine or of The Spirit to show for it. And later, in the end, it destroys them....but for you, do not get tricked "Now." (Jesus said, *"It is The Spirit who gives life; the flesh profits nothing. The words that I speak to you are spirit, and they are life."* John 6:63) (For Study: John 12:42-50) Obey God and see the divine. Suffer, wait, don't give into temptation, it's empty and no power. That is why there is a lot of no power, forms of godliness ministries. It was those either not called or "Called" and gave into temptation to get it "Now." They were not purified in the fire, nor tested, so they have no real ministry. If Jesus had to go through that before His ministry started...what makes you better? And it can't be that you pick your own fire. It will happen by God's timing, and will, if you are "Called". You just surrender. It will be real and in the end, you will not be destroyed and surrounded by the fake, powerless. You have to say, no matter what, "God's will be done." Just like Jesus in the garden, don't avoid the cross, His will be done. If you never get a church, if you are never "seen", if whatever.... God's will be done. The real, for you, your family and everyone else, it is worth it. The only way for you to "Learn" the things in the school of God, is to have the right heart and you have to pass the tests. Otherwise, no gold. God's wisdom is kept from the "wise" and learned, arrogant. They don't understand the ways of The Spirit. They don't understand God's power. They want to "learn" it, so they can get the glory for it but God will not share His glory with another. (*"I am The Lord, that is My Name; And My glory I will not give to another..."* Isaiah 42:8) You are not worthy, only He is. You just have to receive. Believe & Receive, by His will and guiding alone. He will keep it from the "wise" & the "learned" and reveal it to babes. You do not get "The Divine" outside of God's will and without carrying "The Cross."

So as there was attack, God would continue to divinely intervene & encourage with a Word. One night before leaving to go to college. (my 1st year at Brownsville) The Spirit of The Lord came down with a special Word and I did not realize how important this Word would become at the end of the same school year. As I was going to bed, I was in bed reading my Bible and praying, just before going to sleep. When all of the sudden, Mom & Dad, surprisingly just came in the room. They were all touched and teary. Mom said, "I was just reading this, and The Lord touched me...I feel it's for you....The Lord has just been touching us about it!" She read 2 Timothy 1:11 *"And of this Gospel I was appointed a herald and an apostle and a teacher. That is why I am suffering as I am......"* She said *" We feel you are Appointed!"* "Look, and see, that it says....why you are *suffering as you are....That is why you are suffering as you are!, You are Appointed....You are Appointed.....Appointed.....!!!"* She was touched and crying, it was a God thing. They prayed for me. We were touched. We knew it was God. Awesome. Then after we were winding down. I went out into the kitchen, (mind you, this is about 11 o'clock at night now...) I walked out to get some cereal..... And mom followed. Dad was there also, sitting in the kitchen and Mom got touched again,...crying and shouting...... *"You're Appointed..... Appointed.....Appointed.....You are Appointed!!!!"* Wow, so we were all touched, we knew it was The Spirit of God! Thank You Lord, for again confirming my "Call" and office to which you have "Appointed" me. The next day, as I was standing by my TV in my room. I saw a sign, that I hadn't really noticed...Until now. It was a little sign that had what "Seth", my name means in Hebrew. Guess what it means?? Yep, ready...... "Appointed." I was amazed, I showed mom. We were in amazement. How awesome! So now, everything was easy, and going to be easy right? Wrong. Remember a lot of times, He speaks for a reason. So what is the very thing that you think, the devil would speak through jealous, evil people? Yep... Things said later...,That would challenge the word, making it like it wasn't God. That it was flesh.

(That's how they are, a lot of times they falsely accuse you of the way they are. They fleshly call themselves, and make up words from God etc..) Challenging being able to be in ministry or to be able to be a leader etc....on and on.. Not once, not twice but constant. Listen, be sure, if there is so much attack saying it's not God....that's one thing you can be sure...it is God! Because the devil & people don't care if it's flesh "Called." They get hyped up and it is fine with everyone. The flesh is always fine with everyone. As Jesus said, *"Woe to you when all men speak well of you, For so did their fathers to the false prophets."* (Luke 6:26) Be careful if everyone thinks well of you, fleshly. If not everyone, and church leaders didn't like Jesus and had a problem with Him, what makes you better? What do you think people will do with you, who are truly "Called", walking in God's will for your life, carrying The Cross?

As I would come home, my 1st trip home that semester, I had a powerful Word as I was praying and a divine appointment. So as we made plans, as I was flying home my flight got changed. I had to fly into and land through a hurricane. I had called and left my mom a message. I didn't know if she got it, she had to change my flight. I was praying and ran to the other flight, got there just in time. Mom had got my message, changed my tickets and I was on the plane. Whew....that was close. But I believe all by design. You never know, through prayer, when your day is messed up, that it just might be God orchestrating a divine appointment and getting your attention. As I prayed on my flight home, I was enjoying The Lord. Then I got touched. As The Lord started to touch me, I saw like a picture.....like a vision, I saw myself hugging a loved one and asking God to breathe on them. It was powerful. Then when I landed, because of the switched flight, I was all discombobulated....threw me out of wack a little. While trying to get my bearings, I had a divine appointment...(Father Virtue Story)

Father Virtue
(10/16/99)

It was fall break at Brownsville. When I went to the airport, the plane that I was supposed to take was delayed for four hours or indefinite. I was supposed to fly to New Orleans to BWI. However, there was no other flight to New Orleans that would land in time to catch my other plane. It was a big ordeal to get all the money arrangements. I ended up catching a plane to Jacksonville to BWI. The airlines were worried that I could not fly to Jacksonville because a hurricane was coming in. I had to leave a message with Mom telling her to get the flight money to my new flight. Not knowing if she got the message, I landed at 12 noon in Jacksonville with my next flight taking off at 12:15. Luckily, my Mom got the message and I was able to get on my flight. I landed in BWI 2 hours before I told my awesome friends to pick me up. Then I went to the baggage claim wondering what I was going to do. While I started making phone calls, of all the people there, a priest caught my eye. It went through my mind that I'd like to talk to him and find out what his beliefs were. I heard my name paged, but I didn't know where to go, so I went over to the priest to ask him. He said he wasn't sure so I went to an information phone and he followed me-weird huh! I was to call my Mom. The priest followed me again this time to a pay phone. While I was calling, it started going through my mind to be kind to strangers for in doing so, you're entertaining angels. I really started wondering if this priest was an angel, I was really looking at him. After I got off the phone, he said he needed help calling somebody. To get my attention, he said my name and it startled me. While I was thinking how does he know my name, he said, "I heard you say it before." He said his name is "Father Virtue." That's all he said. After I got through making all my calls, I started helping him make calls. I tried for a while. I asked him if he knew his home phone number, and he said he didn't know. How could he not have known it? He went to say he didn't have any money and needed a ride to Frederick. I was thinking in my head,"Lord, if this is an angel I have money and I can take him." It was so strange. Anyway, he said, "I'll try." He dialed a couple numbers, and got the wrong number. Then he said he was gonna try a number just strictly from memory and finally got through. While he was talking, I kept saying in my mind if this is an angel, then who is he talking to? When I said that in my mind, he leaned over and acted like he was gonna let me listen, then pulled the phone back. After that, I asked him,"What's that book you got?" He said it was a book for his class and that he was a teacher of Catholic Theology. I told him I was going to a school of ministry. He said," Wow, thank heavens." So we got to talking and I started telling him about the revival and how the Lord was moving and how people were getting saved. He asked, "Well, who's the leader of that?" I said, "That's what's cool. There's a pastor and he lets other people minister so no man can get the glory." I started telling him what the Lord was dealing with, with me with stuff, like putting Him first and just having a relationship with Him before anything else, before ministry just to be in love with the

Lord. I told him that people don't need new sermons or good songs. We need the power! I told him about the burden on Pastor to pray to break denominations and I said, "That's true, because there's only one heaven and one Jesus and one Bible. We need to let the Lord do whatever He wants to be led by the Spirit. I said that when the power comes, no one can say anything. I told him about my testimony, about the Lord touching me when I was 5 and he thought it was awesome and agreed with everything I was saying. He said, "It sounds like the prophets in the Bible and how they were "called" at a young age." He said, "The Lord's got something for you." I told him, "Because of what the Lord spoke to me, to "Be good and pray every day" and I told him I could probably count on my hand how many days I've missed without praying." He said, " You make it sound so clear and I can normally tell when someone knows what they're talking about. Judging by your family history, and how you are "called", I feel like the Lord is going to use you. I could probably count on my hand how many people that I've met like you." He said, "I'm going to tell my students about you, and I wish you could come and speak." He said that he had been worried about the younger generation, and that it was amazing to see how someone my age could talk so clear, and that he felt better. At different times in our conversation, I could tell that he was touched and sometimes I could feel the Lord. He said, "You're not worried or intimidated, about me being a teacher of theology and an old clergyman to talk to me, are you?" And I shook my head no. I said, " I felt gypped by the church, because I never knew I could have the power in my life. I told him about communing with the Lord and how real it can be, and the church didn't tell me it could be this way. I said," We are free, not just the "la, la, la same old thing, we can just talk to the Lord." I told him about my heart problems, and different stuff like with my family serving the Lord. While I was talking in the middle of the airport, my eye caught someone else walking towards us, but I forgot about it and just kept talking to the priest. That same person- a girl came up beside us. It was the same person that was picking him up. He made a joke. He said to the girl, "Do you know what this person is doing? He is witnessing," which means… then I broke in and made a joke and said, "That he needs to get saved." Then everyone laughed; then I added that I was just joking. He said, "Witnessing is sharing their faith about Jesus." As he was explaining to the girl what witnessing was, he said to me, "You don't care about where you go or what you're going to do or about your heart problems." He said, "You've given everything to the Lord, haven't ya?" I nodded yes. He said, "You're just open to the Lord? You've given everything." I nodded "Yes", putting my head down....Then he grabbed my hat and said, "Look me in the eyes, because you've given everything to the Lord, the Lord's gonna give you everything and more. He's even gonna give you Himself." Then he said, "Do you want to pray?" I said, "Yeah." He bowed his head and put his hands together. Then I took my hat off and placed my hand on his shoulder, and I prayed, "Lord, just bless him and fill him Lord. Lord, we don't want religion, we want you!" He said, "I am kind of the older generation, and I am not used to this, but I have seen my students (younger priests) doing that." Then after that, he placed his hand on my shoulder and then he prayed for me, placing his hand on my shoulder. At the end of the prayer, I heard my name being paged, but he didn't want to let me go, and

53

so we talked a little more. Finally, my name was paged again and I said I gotta go, and he said, "Thanks," but with heartfelt gratitude. He didn't realize what he was saying to me, when he said, "You've given your all." Because I feel that I have had to give it all to the Lord. That, that is what the Lord has asked of me, so nothing can taint His gospel, so that only He can get all of the glory, and I can just flow with whatever the Holy Spirit, for whatever the Lord wants me to do...It has been a process of what the Lord has been doing with me, for years...

So as I was picked up by my friends. I shared with them, in amazement, the divine appointment. So I made it home. Not long after being home, (the one I saw myself praying over), stopped around, distraught. I was wondering if this is the time to pray with them like I saw. "God do you want me to pray....?" I was praying, but I didn't. I wasn't sure but I was praying about it. So the next day while sitting in church, I wasn't in the service very much, and I just started to pray and man.... out of the blue God hit me. I started shaking and crying, interceding for that same one I saw. I was asking The Lord, "What? Were they in an accident,...is there something wrong?? What is it??" God said "No".... "Just pray!".......so I did, I couldn't stop. So touched. I heard Dad say to Mom as I was just touched and praying....he said "That's God. That's The Lord touching him." I was having "church" in church. (Sometimes people are so blind, they don't know when the Spirit shows up in the church, they are lost if it's not flesh and will get offended at The Spirit.) So after the service was over, a little while, we got into the car. We were quiet but I knew Mom & Dad were wondering what was up. So I said what happened and I said that was for "A person." God wanted me to pray. I don't know what is going on, no accident or anything, I felt led just to pray. So with that Sunday morning,...later on, somehow..... Dad said, "Come here...listen to this..." They learned there was more to the story. That same Sunday morning, about the same time, in different churches.... They said, "A person" got up and was talking, which is rare, and got really touched. Wow. It was a God thing. So the next day "A person" came around and the story came out. Then I said about what I had seen on the plane flying in. I asked, "Would it be alright if I wrap my arms around you and ask God to breathe on you??" (Now just to say, I just don't do this, it better be God.) "A person" said, "Yeah go ahead.." So, I walked over and wrapped my arms around them and started to cry...asking God to breathe on them. Powerful. Little did I know, this was really the final straw, that after this, the separation would be long and terrible. That this was not a strengthening and starting point but rather a turning away. How, you might ask? You see, little compromises, little sin that you don't take care of will grow. Until, it's done huge damage. People want to believe that if you sin, then repent "quietly" just to God, and not make things right nor stop your sin actions, then it's the same. Wrong, this is a twist and a lie. Yes, God can forgive you, but there are consequences, things are never the same. When you willfully choose to sin and honestly, not truly make it right and stop your actions, then there are lasting consequences. People say about no one is perfect in the Bible, yeah, that's right but....we are to learn from them, not justify sin and copy them in sin. And there are those who did live right. Joseph, Daniel, Job, Ruth, Esther, and many others. Yeah not perfect, but lived right, for The Lord their whole lives. Let them be the example, you want to be. And keep your eyes on Jesus. <u>By God's grace, He can keep you living right, if you do your part.</u> (For Study: Jude 1:24, Hebrews 12:14, Matthew 5:48) And no sin is OK, but there is a difference between short-comings and SIN that separates you from God, that is clearly spelled out in the Bible. The Bible says in 1 John 5:16, *"If anyone sees his brother sinning a sin which does not lead to death, he will ask, and He will give him life for those who commit sin not leading to death. There is sin leading to death. I do not say that he should pray about that."* & in John 13:10, Jesus said to Peter, *"He who is bathed needs only to wash his feet, but is completely clean; and you are clean, but not all of you."* (See sin that sep-arates, 1 Corinthians 6:9-11) 1 John 3:7-9 says, *"Little children, let no one deceive you. He who practices righteousness is righ-teous, just as He is righteous. He who sins is of the devil, for the devil has sinned from the beginning. For this purpose the Son of God was manifested, that He might destroy the works of the devil. Whoever has been born of God does not sin, for His seed remains in him; and he cannot sin, because he has been born of God."* And also, Hebrews 10:26-27 says, *"For if we sin will-fully after we have received the knowledge of the truth, there no longer remains a sacrifice for sins, but a certain fearful expec-tation of judgment, and fiery indignation which will devour the adversaries.* (For Study: Hebrews 6:6, Hebrews 10:29-31) Don't be around people and ministries that don't believe you can live right, because then you won't, you will not have the power or doctrine to live right. Be around the real, that preaches you can be completely set free, when we completely surrender to Him. Scriptures say in Luke 4:18 *"The Spirit of The Lord is upon Me, Because He has anointed Me To preach the gospel to the poor;*

He has sent Me to heal the brokenhearted, To proclaim liberty to the captives And recovery of sight to the blind, To set at liberty those who are oppressed; To proclaim the acceptable year of The Lord." Get the Truth because the truth, will set you Free, to not stay bound and depressed in sin. He came to set the captives free. That's the Good News, not that you stay bound but can be set free.

(Side Note: If you're on your own not led by The Spirit, pushing, manipulating and opening your own doors etc...it will never be of The Spirit or real ministry that will last. No matter how it's received it is not real and always against The Lord. Flesh is always against and deceiving away from and stealing from The Spirit. Flesh is never satisfied and always needs all the attention and always promoting self. Held accountable for deceiving away from the real. Flesh think those of The Spirit are like them, (All competition) because they do not understand The Spirit-led and how God opens the doors and moves; when it's Him.)

So, there was much damage done after this turning point decision. See, it came by the way of God giving people chances. He gives people chance after chance to repent, to stop, to change. Then if they don't and won't hear, things get worse. They try to add themselves into the miracle and actually short circuits the miracle from coming about and tries to destroy who God uses. Jealousy is terrible. When people are jealous the Bible says, *"Against jealousy, who can stand?"* Just like as old as Cain and Abel, jealousy comes in because people don't listen to God's way. They are in the flesh and if you are doing it God's way...they hate it. Rather then repent and do it God's way themselves....they end up wanting to kill you. One time while home, I could just feel the attack against me, it's like witchcraft. I said it to my parents and all I could do was just lay there on the living room floor. I could really feel it. It was affecting me. I could feel the stabbing attack and heaviness. I said, "I can just feel the attack, like people talking about me"....like arrows. We prayed, and all I could do is just lay there on the living room floor. I found out the next day, by a little "Birdie"....that some people had gathered together and were really talking bad about me. Saying all kinds of evil about me. (Now, stop right here...why would anyone allow that...even if it is something wrong..which it wasn't...why all the slander & such?) Anyway I said, "Did you say something? My defense?" Then they got mad at me. Listen....if you allow it, then you are just as guilty of it. People don't even try with me, it's like they just know. I don't accept junk and if there is something real, we will take care of it the right way...not all behind people's back, evil intent & slander..spreading it all around. How can people allow that, doesn't anyone care about my life? Doesn't anyone care about what's right? For everyone's sake.

It was a rough time. That was my 1st trip home, so I was going back to school. I did not know, it was going to be tough. (See why words from The Lord are so important?) My friends and I were pure. There were false accusations but people know the truth. Makes you wonder, what's in their life if they are trying to make up stuff about you. (A lot of the time, the ones who say do not judge, are the ones who protect sin and attack the righteous.)

So here it was, the last Sunday service before coming home. I was praying for a Word of The Lord; I was desperate. God spoke! As I was really praying, it was towards the end of the service, I was desperate and I kept praying. Then Pastor Kilpatrick got up and said, "I have a word for someone here." He said, *"You have an enemy, it's an intimidating enemy. And she has a jezebel spirit on her. And she has been anointed by hell to cause you havoc! And if you had your way, you would run. But I say this to you, if you would run, you'd be just like David's brothers. When David came, did he not say...is there not a cause? When David came, he did not run. And God used goliath, that very thing, to cata-pult David into his ministry. God is going to take that very thing, that jezebel, and catapult you into higher things. And had she not been there, there would be no fear of God and no new release of God's anointing on you.!"* I continued to pray, I wanted a confir-mation. "Please if it's for me...please confirm it." Pastor Crisco got up and said, (as I was praying...I said, "Lord, you've used him to talk to me before, please confirm it......") Pastor Crisco said, "Look at this scripture. I wanted to share along with what Pastor Kilpatrick was saying......" Guess what scripture he read?? 2 Timothy 1:11..12ish.... Exactly what mom shared at the begin-ning of the year. He said it like her too.... *"And of this gospel I was appointed a herald and an apostle and a teacher. That is why I am suffering as I am."* And he emphasized.... *"See that last part, That is why I am <u>suffering as I am</u>."* I knew it was God. I thanked Him for speaking and confirming His word. I was in tears. I des-perately needed it and He spoke. I knew I had to go home and face it and endure the onslaught that was to come.

I came home to what would be the worst summer I ever had. Two & three times a week, I would hear all kinds of derogatory things against me. I would try to just calm it down, would try not to get into anything. Keep it as minor as possible, but there was no appeasing. Remember God speaks a lot of times to sus-tain you through the task He asks you to do, because He knows it's going to be hard. It was. It's hard to explain. Because it's not just a person, flesh and blood, but demonic. (demonic oppression & attack.... a "spirit" of attack. The unseen attack that is hard to explain, unless you have felt it or feel it.) And even though I knew it, it was still painful and I could feel the cutting. Feel the stabbing. I knew it was anointed by the devil to cause me havoc, as the word said. It's hard to explain the "unseeable" pain. The "unseeable" price. The undercutting. The cursing, that carries weight, you feel it. You see the effects of people leaving you, you have the attack affecting your mind and how you think about yourself etc. It's worse for those who are truly "Called." There is more of a price that normal Christians don't understand. Theirs is one level, but common sense would tell you...how much more so, for those "Called" and used by God. Those who God wants to be leaders of the church. (If the devil can get the head of the church, look at all he can destroy or get fake, watered down teaching to. If he can destroy the truly "Called" leaders of the church or get them to compromise, or get them to run or bow,so much can he deceive and destroy.) Listen, and be there for them, they are carrying a greater price. But by God's grace, you can never bow to that, no matter what false accusation they throw at you. A scripture that helped me in this time, when you are in the battle, things are revealed that you never saw or understood before. Matthew 5:10-12 says, *"Blessed are those who are persecuted for righteousness' sake, For theirs is the kingdom of heaven. Blessed are you when they revile and persecute you, and say all kinds of evil against you falsely for My sake. Rejoice and be exceedingly glad, for great is your reward in heaven, for so they persecuted the prophets who were before you."*

How the jezebel spirit works...(Good Bible study subject) It all starts, when you start to tolerate her & in the church. (Revelation 2:20-23 *"Nevertheless, I have this against you: You tolerate that woman jezebel, who calls herself a prophet. By her teaching she misleads my servants into sexual immorality and the eating of food sacrificed to idols. I have given her time to repent of her immorality, but she is unwilling. So I will cast her on a bed of suffering, and I will make those who commit adultery with her suffer intensely, unless they repent of her ways. I will strike her children dead. Then all the churches will know that I Am He who searches hearts and minds, and I will repay each of you according to your deeds."*) She'll be evil and play the victim. Everyone feels sorry for them and they are the ones doing all the lying, etc. She uses anything and everything. Everyone. She falsely accuses, uses immorality, division, peer pressure, threats, trying to hold sin against you and if they can't find sin, will make it up and falsely accuse you, while also excusing all others and their own sin. They will tear others down and belittle, to lift themselves up. They want No competition...on and on, but everything is a competition to them. Everything. To belittle you, they want complete control and if they don't get it, they are going to make you pay. They are insecure. They have to have complete control. They say "forgiveness" to protect their sin. You have to let them alone, to be able to destroy everyone or you're not forgiving, or loving... etc. Lie, lie, lie. Then they say they are the truth and even in ministry. A "prophetess." She (jezebel) hates especially the prophets of God and wants to kill the real and then turn and be a fake one. She uses everyone. She uses weak-willed people. Manipulates everything. Gets people to do her bidding. Whatever it takes. It doesn't matter if you know she lies etc. Just as long as the outcome is what she wants. She will accuse you of the way she is, to slander you, protect her and what she is actually doing. A complete hypocrite. But even people who know it, are too scared to stand against it, so they "tolerate" her. For her sake and everyone else's, stand against it. Don't let someone else be singled out and killed. Stand. Don't tolerate it, no matter what they scream. Until it is completely stopped and no more junk. (This foul spirit can use men as well and also uses many times, the second in authority, to turn the head of the main authority. A spouse, a secretary, a vice president, or spouse of the one in charge to manipulate and control everything. Too insecure to lead but take credit for success but blame leader if it doesn't work.) Walked out repentance, by their fruit you will know them, not talk, but walked out truth.

Remember I am talking about the Truly "Called", one of the main things the church needs in this day & hour & the last days, is discernment, to know how to combat the false doctrines & false demonic spirits. This is so that you are not bound by them in things that seem right but are completely wrong, against The Spirit and protects the false. The false protects the false. The devil himself masquerades as an angel of light. Discern between the True & false, flesh & Spirit. I started to realize all the more, again, this scripture for me, *"Blessed are those who are persecuted for righteousness' sake, For theirs is the kingdom of heaven. Blessed are you when they revile and persecute you, and say all kinds of evil against you falsely for My sake. Rejoice and be exceedingly glad, for great is your reward in heaven, for so they persecuted the prophets who were before you."* But the other side is, *"Woe to you when all men speak well of you, for so did their fathers to the false prophets."* Woe to you,....that's a big difference & a sure sign between the real & the false. It's not OK if people are persecuting the real. Don't use this scripture as a justification against God's "Called." It's sin to speak against God's "Called." *"Touch not God's Anointed and do My prophets no harm."* Psalms 105:15. Fear God...not jezebel....who teaches not to fear God, to speak against & try to kill God's Anointed. On the "Called's" part you're blessed but on their part it is sin and they will be held accountable. It's not "OK" for the "Called" to be persecuted nor "Without Honor" in his own hometown. Don't tell the "Called" this, in allowance of it, tell the wicked to stop sinning and Honor God's truly "Called".

Now into my 3rd semester, I had to get my own apartment because of some "troublemakers". So now I was continuing school. It seemed peaceful to start, but the devil again would continue to harass. It was this semester that I had three of my A's, that I had for some of my classes, were changed to F's. My attendance at this time was also completely erased, wiped out. Also, my parents were coming down and had an appointment to fix my grades that were wrongfully changed. So as we were in there correcting my grades, the guy says, "Yeah, we had a guy that had his attendance wiped out!" I said, "Yeah, that was me!" He was shocked. And I was like, thinking to myself, "Anybody think something fishy is up?" There was a new president, that was the one that had given my special word. So, I had prayed about meeting that new president. I wanted to share the special word with him. I also put down on the paper that I was going to give him, some things that I felt still needed corrected. This is all through prayer. So it worked out. I was able to meet with him. I shared The Word of The Lord, that he was used to give to me and he said, "Yeah, I remember that word." It went good. He then said, "I can tell in my spirit, that you have great discernment and can probably feel things on campus still, that need corrected." I said, "Yeah, that's why I wrote those three things on the back of the paper that need corrected." He was surprised, and said, "I didn't even see that, I will look at that." It went good, but not long after, things changed drastically. To make a long story short, with false accusations and mistreatment, I ended up going home. I would pray and didn't understand all this. All you can do sometimes is just keep standing. So, as things went on I would just keep praying and standing. Scriptures say in Ephesians 6:13, *"And after you have done everything, to stand."*

Chapter 5

Finding The Right One

The coming together....The "Non-Talk."

I had always prayed for the right one, or to find the right one to marry...But how? I needed a miracle. There was no one around, I would pray & want God's will. I want someone who loved God, living right, not ugly..But Nice looking. But me being so picky...God, How? Who? As I prayed one night & talking to God I said, "There is just no one around..." I was proud of not having any serious relationships. But I was now 22 yrs. old; this is starting to get serious. I need to find someone. Little did I know, in fact, I came to learn I knew nothing. God had already prepared *Someone* for Me, (who was going through her own testing & preparation), who was already around me. She would be a God ordained match for my Heart & to be able to be used by God in the ministry. The same month that God was finally bringing us together, down in Florida, was the same month back home that it was put on the christian radio station a commercial saying at the end of it, "Don't date your best friend, don't date your best friend's friend and whatever you do...don't date a guy by the name of Seth!" Wow, can you believe that?! Crazy?! See we were not saying anything about our relationship, completely a secret (because we didn't know ourselves). And some people, that knew how Kendra was feeling, tried to lie, cause division and get her away from me. Lie to her, knowing what she was thinking, that she felt it was The Lord for us (I didn't know anything...lol). But when she was around me, she never saw any of those lies, that people would say about me. Why? Get a life. Jealousy is unbelievable! You're messing with and trying to ruin people's lives. Kendra & Seth, two of about the most picky people, finally, The Lord, worked it out. A miracle!! In spite of all the evil and lies, God still worked it out. When we came home and told our parents, about our relationship, my Dad said, "It's on the radio!" I was like, "What?!" I thought he was kidding but it was real. We didn't even know ourselves, nor Mom & Dad. And we had just started to get together and people, so obsessed, put it on the radio?! The devil knew. And people still didn't quite know, but they were scared and jealous.

So, how did we get here? Glad you asked...lol. It all started when I was 20 years old & in my third year of college at ACC. The beginning of the year I felt led, that I wanted to start taking my Bible to school & one that was clearly seen from the outside, that it was a Bible. So as I walked into my class, little did I know... that this was a life changing event...because there was a girl I had never met in the upper deck of chairs. This girl was finding out, because God had confirmed & answered a simple small prayer, she had prayed two nights before. (This was the prayer she prayed after seeing me at a football game. She went home and before bed prayed, "Lord, if it is Your will, let me talk to him." She had never prayed anything like that before. When she first saw me at the football game, I was sitting a few seats in front of her, she thought I was cute, (yes sir..lol) watched how I was and felt like she could tell I was a Christian. So after she prayed and went to bed, she forgot about her prayer.) Two days later, I walked in her class carrying my Bible. It was a God thing!

After class, I had a girl come up & introduce herself saying, "Excuse me, I see you are carrying your Bible, do you know if there are any Christian clubs on campus?" I told her that there is a youth group I am a part of & I lead the worship. Anyway, when I got home, I told Mom the incident that had just happened & said, "Isn't that cool! I just started taking my Bible and this girl just came up and asked about it and about a Christian club, etc."

That was the 1st day I had started carrying my Bible & someone ask about it. (Mom never forgot that "incident" but kept it in her heart.) By the way her maiden name was Kendra "Goodpaster". Isn't that funny? So as time went on, as we were friends, I would think, "That would be a cool way to meet my wife,...too bad that was with Kendra." lol. Again, I was clueless to the hints God kept giving me.

("If you want the top, don't settle for the slop...wait for God's one! Perfect for you and how He will work it out.")

As I prayed that prayer at Night, for the right one and after years of knowing her...

All of the sudden...As I prayed...God dropped her Name on Me, out of the blue. I said, "Her?" Then I shook it off & bewildered, (lol) & I went to sleep..wondering... Then came my 23rd birthday. My party was already celebrated the day before. But this was my actual birthday & Kendra & only Kendra stopped by after church & gave me a card. As my parents, Kendra & I sat downstairs in the T.V. Room, the most crazy, ridiculous thought, went through my mind..looking at her across from me... (Never thinking This way ever.) "If she would be the one to be My wife, that would be alright with me!" What? What was I thinking...again shaking it off...I am Mr. Cool? What in the world was I thinking?

I would come to find out later, someone's prayers were working, providing a way, making preparations for the future. I also came to find out much later, that very same night before Kendra came over, that Kendra had knelt at the altar that night, praying for God to speak to her, she was wanting to do the right thing, whether to go away to school or not or stay & finish her nursing & she heard the soft whisper, of The Lord, *"You are precious, you are precious, you are precious."* 3 times. As she got up & went back to her seat, a lady came over, not knowing what The Lord had just spoke to her & said, "I feel God wanted me to tell you, "*You are precious*!" God was working with Kendra & He was working on me.

God is the matchmaker. He has matched people long before dating sites & anything else and His matches last. He is love, He knows the Heart & He knows you. And only He can fix, the right exact & only one, that fits your heart.

> *"For this reason a man shall leave his father and mother and be joined to his wife, and the two shall become one flesh; so then they are no longer two, but one flesh. Therefore what God has joined together let no man separate."* Mark 10:7-9

The Bible says, *"He created them male and female, and blessed them and called them mankind in the day they were created."* Genesis 5:2

It is Holy and to be saved for each other.

Anything perverted or unnatural, impure, is not God's way. In spite of what the world says it is destruction & hurts everyone. It will separate you from God and His blessing cannot rest on sin & therefore will not work. Marriage is between, one man and one woman for life. To sin sexually, sins against your own body. Perversion, affects not only you spiritually, but also physically as well. As The Bible says in Romans 1:27 and sinning against your own body, 1 Corinthians 6:18. (For Study: Romans 1, 1 Cor. 5 & 6)

Marriage is a picture of our relationship with God. (side note: We both wore white & had lines in our vows saying (we were) pure, kept for each other & the day of our wedding. We especially wanted all that, because of the false accusations. And we were proud of our testimony!)

He is coming back for a spotless Bride, without spot or wrinkle. He sees us as His bride.

As you want someone clean, so you be clean; with your eyes, body & save yourself for the one God has for you. Also, how God wants you, reserved, for Him. Be the way you want your spouse to be. Man needs to love & take care of his wife, not in goofy ideas of man's wisdom, but in God's ways...just Truth. 1 John 3:18 says, *"Dear children, let us not love with words or speech but with actions and in truth."* The Word of God, not man's ideas, the same as man's rules on dating or whatever, nothing is OK... out of God's will. You don't date just to date, but be picky. Not date, but wait on God's timing. (Note: Anyone can get someone...

you don't want just "someone"..You want the "One" God has for you.... The only way for it to truly work out... get God's one!)

When Kendra was getting her nursing, she would love when I would come home from being away at school. (She had it bad... lol) I would learn she would be praying & I love it, "Lord, I want to be with the right one, I want him to be with the right one, but I don't want anyone else if it can't be him." Wow, what a prayer. I like it!

I remember saying, "My wife is only going to have eyes for me..." Little did I know, my future wife heard that, she was there in the room and liked it. So watch what you say, you never know if your future spouse can hear it! Lol Be the kind of person you want your spouse to be...picky...saving your eyes & heart for The Lord first...then for the ONE, God has for you. You don't want it if it's not God. Wait For The Lord, it's worth it. It's not worth it not to. As long as you do His will, you can't miss. He will work it perfectly! Other than salvation, it is your biggest life decision. He has the ONE for you....(Trust no one else.)

So here we were at Bible school, how did we get here? Well, after Kendra prayed at church, and after the summer, after my birthday, we were headed back to school and Kendra felt led to enroll. After a time, and also our friend could not enroll yet,.. soooo, it was just Kendra and I, down there in Florida. So, after a time of us being there, something was just bothering me about her. It kept bothering me and bothering me. So, I didn't say anything to her, but I started Fasting about it. And after fasting days about it, it seemed to just keep getting worse.... Why is this so annoying, why is she bothering me? I felt like she was hiding something...What is it? I was miserable.... People also down there kept harassing us about being friends. It kept getting worse. Finally I said, "You are bothering me so much I can't take it, I feel like you are hiding something from me...what is it??" I said, "If you have to fast about it.... fast!" She said, "I am fasting!!" Both of us were fasting about something and didn't know the other one was. I can't help but think God was just up there smiling and laughing at the discomfort because He knew what was coming and what He was pushing us toward..... Our Now Famous..... "Non-Talk!!" Only God could work it out this way, with all the signs and how I about needed hit over the head! Clueless! Lol. So we, as "friends".. went to go bowling and ended up, we stopped in the car... and was going to get to the bottom of what is going on.....and it was going to be the biggest, "Non-Talk" ever, that changed our life! We sat there and I would say, "I feel like you are hiding something.." She said and would say, "Well, I could tell you something that might help, but...." And she would look out the window, then look back at me with love in her eyes.... and say, "Don't you know?!" "Ohhh, You don't know?!" So, looking out the window and back again, after a little bit of this.... I said, (after dummy, me, it started to dawn on me...lol, and with a cool look...) "Well, I think I know...!!" She was like, man you're making this hard...lol "Well, I think I know..." "Do you know, you think it's The Lord?" She with love in her eyes, slowly would nod like.... you, dummy yes.... In her head she had always thought of how it would be, that she prayed for years, everyday and she would surprise me with letting me know, and yet, this is the way it's happening. (She told me later, that for years, she would actually practice saying to me how she had prayed to meet me and would think how surprised I would be.) And me with the signs I had and all the fasting.... without officially asking out or saying anything out loud.... Our "Non-Talk"..... I took her hand, and without officially saying anything..... We prayed together. And from there our relationship grew. Only God could've worked it out this way and we wouldn't want it any other way!

Marriage God's Way......Ephesians 5:22-33 *"Wives, submit to your own husbands, as to The Lord. For the husband is head of the wife, as also Christ is head of the church; and He is the Savior of the body. Therefore, just as the church is subject to Christ, so let the wives be to their own husbands in everything. Husbands, love your wives, just as Christ also loved the church and gave Himself for her, that He might sanctify and cleanse her with the washing of water by the word, that He might present her to Himself a glorious church, not having spot or wrinkle or any such thing, but that she should be holy and without blemish. So husbands ought to love their own wives as their own bodies; he who loves his wife loves himself. For no one ever hated his own flesh, but nourishes and cherishes it, just as The Lord does the*

church. For we are members of His body, of His flesh and His bones. "For this reason a man shall leave his father and mother and be joined to his wife, and the two shall become one flesh." This is a great mystery, but I speak concerning Christ and the church. Nevertheless let each one of you in particular so love his own wife as himself, and let the wife see that she respects her husband."

This is marriage God's way, the only way it will work. If you want your way, it won't work. Some of the problem is, Pastors are not submissive to The Lord, so wives are not submissive to their husbands. It's all rebellion. It trickles down. If you do not have true submission to The Lord or His word, then how do you expect others to be submissive the way they should be and kids the way they should be? Kids are to obey their parents in The Lord, with a promise, that things will go well with them and that they may live long on the Earth. And fathers are not to exasperate their children, less they become discouraged. It must be real, you must be real. It must be built on The Rock of God's truth in obedience, not religion. It must be protected and stayed on The Rock. Spirit & Not Flesh.

...Marriage, it's a picture of how He sees us. We are His Bride. He is The Bridegroom. And He is coming back for a spotless Bride, a Bride without spot or wrinkle, pure, saved for Him; A Bride that is looking for his appearing and one that loves Him. That's who He is coming for. Do you love Him? Do you long for His appearing?

For marriage, we need Godly instruction. Holy women to teach the younger women, how to act, how to dress. Etc. Same as holy men, fathers, to teach the young men, how to be. The

Bible says, *"You, however, must teach what is appropriate to sound doctrine. Teach the older men to be temperate, worthy of respect, self-controlled, and sound in faith, in love and in endurance. Likewise, teach the older women to be reverent in the way they live, not to be slanderers or addicted to much wine, but to teach what is good. Then they can urge the younger women to love their husbands and children, to be self-controlled and pure, to be busy at home, to be kind, and to be subject to their husbands, so that no one will malign the word of God. Similarly, encourage the young men to be self-controlled."* Titus 2:1-6

Godly instruction: in order to wait for the right one to marry and how to have a successful healthy marriage once you have found the right one. And we need those with successful marriages to teach. We need those examples to be the ones teaching God's foundation in order to have more families in God's blessing. In the end, truly that's what you want. A Godly family, only found in God's will and through prayer. Pray together. Keep the sin and snakes out. Put The Lord first and rely on Him. He will guide you. Don't go by the lies and false appearances of the world. It will not last and is not as it appears. God's way only, is what you want. He wants to give it, but it has to be His way and He will bless you!

(Pray and surrender all, right now, to find the right one to marry. And also, pray right now and bless your marriage and family, to be God's way....In Jesus Name!)

Chapter 6

First Assignments Ministry: Planting The Church & Birth of SWMI

W ell, I could not believe I was on my way home, & glad to be coming home. As bad as it was, God would defend me; but I always would want more defense. The attack would continue, but we kept moving forward by The grace of God. Just like with Paul's thorn, God's Grace did not deliver him right then, but helped him through the hard places. God uses it to keep you relying on Him, so He can use you powerfully. As God told Paul, *"My Grace is sufficient for you, for My Power is made perfect in weakness."* 2 Corinthians 12:9. So that in weakness, God's power can rest on you. When we are weak, He is strong. So Paul was used powerfully. Let me say this right here & correct another false twist on this, for the "allowers" of sin. Weakness here is not "Sin" in his life, it was a thorn in his flesh, to kill flesh so he can be used in the Spirit. To keep him humble and relying on God, for God's Glory. When you're in the false and no power, you see everything through the eyes of allowing sin rather than repentance & deliverance from sin. They can't live right, because of lack of surrender to whatever God wants. Without The Cross and true repentance;

you get a false gospel, that makes it "OK" to live in sin. It attacks anyone that comes along and says, "You can be set free...." and they say, "Grace" but if you're living by Grace, Grace is power to be set free & live free, not a license for sin.

So as we continued on, I worked & finished school through Berean online school. I got my Ministry degree and also got my Certificate of Ministry in the Assemblies of God. As soon as I received my license, we celebrated, knowing it was a miracle! God opened two doors immediately. One was with a Methodist church; an outreach called "The Rock," where 50-60 kids would come out about every Friday night. Then right after that door, an Associate/Youth Pastor position at an Assembly of God church opened. During that time, was when the kids from the outreach started coming to the church. Some got filled with The Holy Spirit. We baptized many right there, in water, in a cow trough in The Rock building. They would share their testimony and do skits. About every Friday night for ten months, kids would respond to the altar call to be saved & make things right with God. Amazing and the church "as usual" crowd, would miss what God was doing and try to interfere with the real. I would learn that the church van would purposely, not pick up or skip over the kids, kids that wanted to come to church and would get ready and stand all by themselves waiting to go to church. How is that possible? So, my wife & I started to follow the van and pick up the ones they would skip. This is the whole point of the church, to reach the lost and if they can't come to church, where can they go to be saved? Woe to those who reject those who would want The Lord, so you can just play church. So, I started seeing some of the issues of why so many people can miss out on knowing The Lord and feeling not welcome in church. The fire started to build even more for me to reach the "Un-churched" or "Un-welcome." At this time, with Kendra giving a word of The Lord to the Pastor, praying he makes the right decision,... we had no idea what he was deciding... church packed out and looking for land.... He later announced he was leaving. During this time, I believe the church & former pastor, was thinking I would take over. I was thinking and leaning towards taking it and I believe it would have helped keep the church together but would become a pattern of interference from fill-ins and the like. About this time at a prayer meeting... A lady shared a dream..... Her Dream,

The Wednesday after Easter:

"She had a dream early Sunday morning that, "She was walking in Allegany county with women from the prayer group. Some women had husbands behind them, some women were alone.

We saw a field burnt up and pigs skulls. There was a fence and water all around the burnt field.

Across the water was a green field of grass and deer and Pastor Seth. And Pastor Seth was taking care of the deer.

Then we saw a pig put his nose under the fence and just as the pig touched the water, he was burned-up. Then we knew where the pig skulls came from.

The water, was the living water from the Lord. And the water that separated the burned-up field from the green grassy field was the living water from the Lord."

So after that, about the same time, both doors closed. They both opened & closed at the same time. It lasted about ten months. Amazing.

After this, as I would pray and only want God's will. I would never and do not ever, want to <u>promote myself</u> or <u>open my own doors</u>. Only as I felt it was The Lord after being asked, then I would go. I would be asked to speak at churches or try out for Pastor positions. The church would want me and I would probably have taken it but for some reason; others, who would have nothing to do with it, would hinder it. I would try out for the church, everyone would want me but some people would not allow it or interfere or something. You start to see why some areas remain cold & no real revival. Only if I were flesh, could I get it. I could have a "big" church if I wanted it. But, I don't want it the flesh way...only God's will and way, "big" or "small" & His timing. One of these times, I ministered, it seemed to be a powerful service, many responded. Before this service, I was praying for The Lord to speak to me....and He did. I felt The Holy Spirit speak this to me. It was somewhat of a difficult word. And He said, *"You asked Me...Now this is what I am saying....and if you don't start the service out this way, I will not be with you the rest of the service."* Wow. The word had to deal with "Someone that was abused and God wants to heal you and I think it is a woman, and there is someone also in the church building, somewhere that is in sin, looking at pornography, and if they didn't repent today, their sin is going to be exposed." It was a powerful response to the altar call and afterward, a lady came up to me and said, "That word about abuse, was for me, I was abused." This is the place beforehand I was warned that no one responds and I was really praying about it; seemed dead. The altar was filled. Only God can do that. The board took me and my family out to eat and introduced me as their new pastor. We both wanted me there for the church. After some time I inquired, thinking I was to hear back... and a "person" would not get back to me. So weird. It wasn't long after that, that he, himself, did not have his church anymore. Another time, was when the pastor of the church was leaving and the members of his church, I believe, He and his wife were All expecting and wanted me to be appointed the new pastor. But again, a "person", interfered. (Heard it was said, "If he wants to wait on The Lord, he can wait on The Lord at home.") A church that was once packed out and looking to build, now soon, was closed. This is the problem in areas, deadness gets deadness and gets rid of the real. I will never forget, one of my first assignments, I was asked to give the altar call at a big missions conference, where many church leaders, worship leaders, pastors, evangelists, missionaries etc.. would be in attendance. As I was praying about the service and altar call, again I was told no one ever responds...so it even makes me pray harder. The Lord spoke to me, I wrote it down. It was another tough word, "Lord, how can I share this? Help me..." So as I sat there before the service, the pastor of the church would not even look at me, he would greet everyone but me and Kendra. So, as the time came, I went forward, with the choir behind me and the church full. I stood as one of my first assignments of God and delivered The Word. I obeyed God. You could about hear a pin drop it was so quiet as I delivered The Word. It was about being clean while ministering, to have holy hands. To not being in sin and ministering. To let God have His way and not our own way, which is rebellion and to repent, because He is coming soon and He's coming whether you are ready or not. My wife then sang, a cappella, "In the presence of Jehovah." There were some people that responded, to come to the altar. (Which they said, "No one ever responds...") I want to say right here, I've seen many respond and the altar filled and none respond at times to the altar call. It's not about the response, you want to see All saved, but it's about delivering and throwing out the net for salvation. Then whatever the response, you did what God wanted you to do, and the responsibility is now on the hearers, not you. God gives you free will, you can accept or reject Him, the choice is yours. Afterward, I had only one minister, an older missionary come up and thank me for being obedient. (I said to Kendra, well get the car running, we're gonna want to leave right after this one...lol) You don't want ministers not living right, in sin, spewing out words that make the flock sick, but holy ministers, worship leaders, pastors, evangelists, missionaries, teachers....to help live right and be healthy. Be examples, to make it to heaven. We are responsible for what we allow. By the way, that pastor that did not want to greet us, was later removed from the church. (If the Shepherd is healthy, so will the flock be.)

Season of the radio: The Lord opened it up that we could be on the radio. I loved it. When we first started we were told, "After a couple months the well may run dry." Well, 7 years later, I was still burning. That's the difference between being "Called" and one who is just a hired hand. I don't keep my messages nor do I get them from a book. I would laugh at the commercials that say, "Get the sermons here. It will help." I would say if you have to go there to get sermons, and use old ones, then you're probably not "Called". Because if you are "Called", you get it from The Lord. And it is like a fire shut up in your bones! Get out of the ministry, if you are not "Called" and are using old stuff. We need fresh from The Lord, not of the letter that kills, but Spirit and life, a true feeding. I loved being on the radio. I could get the truth out. Get the real out. We were on many radio stations in the area. I thought there were many that felt the way I did, that wanted to hear about sin and give real altar calls for repentance. Wanted to hear the real about letting The Lord have His way in our churches. To truly worship in Spirit and truth. I did not realize how hardened and rebellious many in the area had become. They did not want to hear about repentance and have true conviction. They like their little church cliques with their little religion. And the ones that were upset, were not going to pay a price to fix it. They did not want to leave their comfy church pew, positions or stand for what they "say" they believe in and go where the truth was preached. They did not want to give up their social, appearance group. Then it becomes a stronghold and an obstruction to those who are truly seeking The Lord. They liked the easiness without the cross. But in the end, sugarcoated preaching deceives, destroys and leads to destruction. But to get the church to wake up, seemed impossible. (But with God all things are possible) So an area is without excuse. I don't want to hear about deadness, if you are unwilling to go and do what God wants. Same as, if God is moving in healing, and you don't want to humble yourself and go where God is moving. If you want your dead religion, your way, you will miss your healing. You miss being set free and family truly getting saved because you want to compromise and play church. You want your way instead of God's way. I learned people were secret likers, but outwardly quiet. Same as those who didn't like it, knew me, but when I would see them out later, would turn away and act like they didn't know me or see me. And it took me a little bit to understand what was going on, then I started to realize, "Oh..... they must have heard me on the radio." And instead of liking it, were offended. People want revival but in a "Nice" way. But that's not how it works. It's God's way without compromise and you may not be liked by everyone. It will not be real without it-real ministry. Nor will God move on an unholy foundation and with sin leadership. He can not use and move with disobedience. It doesn't mean it's perfect, but He knows if you are willing and completely surrendered to Him, and He knows when you're not and if you have secret sin in your life & are not living right. Then to suit their lifestyles they compromise and start to teach false doctrine,which leads many astray and away from the truth. Same as, just not "Going There." "Nobody is perfect..."etc. Right, but they use that as a license to sin and convince you, you can't live right, which is a lie. There are Holy, solid churches. There is power, by God's grace to live right, and that's how you get power to live right, when you completely surrender to Him. It's not your will anymore. If you're living by Grace, then you will have power to live right. Those who say "grace" but are not living right, are not living by grace but that's what's of the law and letter. They have not surrendered to The Lord, and are falsely giving licenses to sin. Wrong! I like to say, "If you completely surrender to Him, then you will be completely set free!" If you don't, don't expect to be set free, you can't be free until you give your life to Christ. Rebellion is doing things your own way, obedience and the answer is doing it God's way. Period. Pick up the cross, lay your life down & be set free... In Jesus Name!!

Side Note: Candy is nice but all candy will make you sick. We need vegetables & some things that are hard to eat at first but if you do, you'll end up liking it & become healthy. Eat all the gospel of The Spirit. The hard & the easy, to become healthy & mature in The Lord. Milk is for babes but meat is for the mature. (For Study: Hebrews 5:12-14)

So, as that went on and we tried going to churches, it always ended up because of pressure by people, and not us, they would try to get us involved. After we would minister, people would really like us and want us to continue to minister. Then, it would always happen that people and even the pastor, would become threatened. We would be hindered. (Jealousy and because it was real. Flesh & Spirit difference.) Then we would end up having to move on. I didn't even care about being up in front. I don't push or promote myself but then they would get us, people would see they liked it, others would get threatened. So it was difficult for us, to find a healthy church, a lot wanted church as usual, half hearted altar calls and would get offended at us just sitting there in the crowd. If we would go somewhere, be quiet and just sit in the crowd, there would be a stirring and we would not be able to stay. We learned we had to and thank The Lord, He led us to start our own church & ministry.

With all of this, The Lord then led us to start a church. <u>Little did I know one of the most powerful Words & signs I would ever get</u>, could come along with some of the worst attack I could have........but God! As we started the church, I thought everyone felt like I did. And with hearing me on the radio for years, would love the truth and talking about letting God have His way. Saying about "sin" and to give altar calls, talking about true worship, revival and on & on. Well, little did I know how "church as usual" people were. How people didn't want to hear about sin & altar calls and didn't care. I did not realize how false doctrine & forms of godliness had taken hold and many wanted the powerless church clubs, programs, shindigs and etc...

Well, the first service came and to my surprise it was just my parents, grandparents, my kids & wife and one other family. I was shocked...hurt...etc...but thank The Lord, He kept me lifted up and would teach me many things through it all. I could grow the numbers, for "numbers" sake, if I wanted, if I would water down the Gospel & tickle ears, but I wanted it God's way. I wanted it real. So as time went on & we pressed in.... The church grew. I am the type of person that if I don't see God moving supernaturally, I start to wonder what's wrong. I had not seen miracles yet, so it led us to pray & fast. It took about six months, then before The New Year as I was driving in my car, The Lord touched me so strong that I felt that I was going to have to pull off the road. He said, *"Keep track of what I AM ABOUT TO DO....."* I did not know exactly what He meant, but I knew that I would listen to what He was telling me to do. I also told the church what I had felt The Lord say. So after the new year, as I was praying and fasting like never before. I will never forget, as we had been praying for prayer requests, and getting ready before the service, a Dad of one of the families in our church said to me, "Guess what?" I said, "What?" He said, "My daughter, got her tests back and her 5 inch cyst that was there, is gone! It disappeared!" Well, needless to say... we were thanking The Lord for the miracle. She was healed. I then started to understand what The Lord meant, so my list started. I started to keep track of what The Lord was doing. Miracles started happening!! People started being healed. (Before all this, one of the times I was recording a radio message, God was just there. Different times when I would record, me and the "Radio Man", my friend, we would get touched. One such time, "Radio Man" prophesied to me. No one was around or knew. He said, "Give me your hands." I gave him my hands and He said, "I feel God is going to use these hands for healing!" He then prayed for me. I wondered about it, thinking awesome. When healings started breaking out, I remembered this word. "Radio Man" was also, later on when I started my job at the hospital, the very first day, my very first ride in the elevator; his son, asked me to come pray for him. "Radio Man" was my very 1st one I got to visit and pray for. It was a God thing.) As the healing count grew, I then thought, when people hear about the healings, they will come. And, what if we get to 10 recorded healings....wow....I know people will be coming, we've never seen it like this, here, not like this...(In our area, this many miracles & healings. My parents and grandparents, who've lived here their whole lives, can testify to that.)...but as miracles happened it is like it would fall on deaf ears. I could not understand. The more I would share the excitement and miracles, the more people would ignore it, not hear or want it. I could not understand why the area would reject the real. The power, miracles, real altar calls, healings, a Christian young family wanting to do what's right. If it's me, I will go to wherever God is moving and whoever He is using. Even if it be a little kid, I would humble myself and go where God is. I just want to be where it's real and God is moving and the truth preached. I could not understand. It is through these times, that is when different scriptures come alive. Like what Jesus would say, "If they reject you, remember they rejected Me first..and if they do not listen to you, shake the dust off your feet..." (For Study: Matthew 10:14-15, James 5:13-16)

After a little time of this, God spoke again. He said, *"I am going to continue to do healings, but be open to other kinds of miracles....."* Two weeks later, other kinds of miracles started to happen.... Some notable Miracles from the church....The Lord did.... and He gets ALL the glory.

Powerful Notable Miracles:

I remember a lady in our church, who was diagnosed with cirrhosis of the liver. An incurable disease. As pastor, I always felt responsible to do all I could do for my flock. So I had it on my heart that week, I was going to fast & pray for her to be healed. So, Monday morning, here we go. I was fasting and going to bombard heaven for her. Well, to my surprise, God was going to save me the whole week, He spoke that morning right away, loud and clear! He said, *"Stop praying for her, she is healed already..."* Wow, I was touched and crying, and there were other words that came with it but I had to wait until next Sunday to deliver them. So, next Sunday came, and I was going to deliver the words of

The Lord. I delivered it, to her and her family's surprise. They were touched. And from that point on she was never dizzy again, she no longer had symptoms. She was healed. The doctor was surprised. She said, "Since that word Sunday morning, All blood work is coming back good and All symptoms have stopped, as of that morning I am healed! My liver is fully functioning." Not only that but, another word for their family came through for the backslidden family member. I told them to tell their family member, God has heard your cry and wants you back home. I was also informed when they told their family member that, he started crying and said for the last two weeks he had been asking God, crying for help. Wow, only God! You see, he had been hurt in the church but, the church is not God, God is God. We serve Him, not people in the church. There were other words, a couple more I wanted to deliver but was not allowed by The Lord. The people, whose miracle was waiting, did not come. Through all this, I learned and would continue to learn that there are testings and chances. There are <u>windows of opportunity</u> that can open and close. People can miss their miracle if they are unwilling to obey God, when & where. And I have to deliver it in God's timing. I had to wait all week, before I was allowed to deliver it. People a lot of times, in a lot of cases, God is seeing if they will do their part, to humble themselves and obey God. To do, sometimes what is uncomfortable, to receive their miracle. Remember, it's His way...not yours. I also learned, that she was told, "To be praying because someone has a powerful word for you this week and it's a hard word to deliver, pray for them." It takes a step of faith. Boy did it. It weighed on me all week. How can I deliver this word? But God! If people are arrogant etc., to me, that is fake, because words of The Lord to me always are heavy, no joke or light. It's serious and carries a price with it.

My wife's eyes....One day, as we were writing down targets for the week, I told Kendra, my wife, that I was going to target her eyes to be healed. She was born with a astigmatism and nearsightedness. Well, we all prayed over our targets all that week. Kendra was praying and fasting in a new way, also that week. As we were driving to church that Sunday morning, my wife starts to say, "Things seem different, things seem clear...." It took her a little bit to realize, as she was putting on her make up in the mirror, and saying the leaves look so clear, I can see the details..... she said, "Oh my gosh....My eyes are healed!!" Wow. She had glasses that she would not wear, rarely would she use them, but would use contacts. But now, she was healed. I said, "You are going to have to share your testimony in front of the church and break those glasses. And She did! Those broken glasses now hang on our wall; a testimony of God's healing power.

(When God moves, it is supernaturally, natural. Not goofy, but real.)

Pastor and his wife, everything is turning around..... During one service, The Lord really started to move. As we were given prayer requests, one was of a pastor's family, with four kids, that had lost everything. Having to move out of their house, lost job, lost ministry etc. In a real bad way. So, we started to pray. Mom, got hit with intercession and started crying out to God, right then, The Lord gave me a word, to give to their friends who were in the service, to deliver to them. I said, "Tell them, everything is turning around for them. You tell them, Everything is turning around!" Powerful. Well, when it's God, it's real! The word was delivered to them. (Who lived in another state) Then, within a couple days later, as the pastor's wife was shopping, a lady came up to her, a stranger, and said while giving her money, "God is saying to you.... Everything is turning around!" Wow. Confirmation and do you know what? Everything turned around! He got a good job, they moved into a new house, he was given a youth ministry position at a church and not only that but got word, back pay was coming to them from the military. Amazing, only God. And with their new youth group & new charter bus, guess the first place they traveled to minister? That's right... Our church. We had a youth conference that was awesome! Only God!

Mom's, ear and 20 yr. back problem healed during worship...... At two separate occasions at our church service during the worship Mom was healed. First, during the service as we worshiped. Mom came sick with an earache, she had cotton in her ear. While we worshiped, as she was worshiping in the back, all of the sudden her ear popped and the cotton ball flew out of her ear and she was healed! And at our other location, when we moved the church. Again, an amazing miracle during the worship, she had a back issue for 20+ years, even struggling that morning, during the worship she felt The Lord heal her, and it has never come back. Awesome! Thank You Lord!

Young girl's mighty healing and anointing oil..... I had seen and saved a certain oil of anointing for her in my bag. She had never come to our church yet, but I had seen, spiritually and God gave me a word that I was to deliver when she came and if she responded to the altar call. Only then could I do what God wanted me to do. It had been over a year, waiting in my bag, never knowing if she would ever come, then finally, one Sunday she came...but I still had to wait to see if she would respond to the altar call, to want to make things right with God. She did, Now was the time.... SO it was not easy what God wanted me to do. I was worried that she could get mad at me, and her first time at our church...but you know me... no matter what, God's will be done... SO I delivered the word to her..... And said this was a sign of what God was saying.... I took the oil and poured it over her head.... The oil reserved for her.....for over a year... To make a long story short, she was delivered and on her way to grow in the Lord. A miracle! And, she loved the oil being poured over her and God's word, that marked her! She said she loved the aroma and did not wash her hair for days! Only God! And I have never done that before or since...It better be God! (I can't believe I did it, but I obeyed God,, and it was a miracle...a lot of times it takes a step of faith, after The Lord speaks it to you! Again, don't try to copy, it is goofy, real goofy in the flesh. Better be God.) Also, an important note. a crucial note, If you want to see the fulfillment of what God has completely promised, you must stay and continue in God's will. If you don't, you can forfeit God's word and will for your life. There are continued words and continued promises IF, you stay in God's will and follow His instructions and not listen to or let the devil or people steal it and trick you out of it. Stay In God's Will, no matter what and you will see His word fulfilled in your life.

Grandma was healed... Mighty woman of faith, My Grandma Higgs, was having some stomach pain. She went to the doctor's and they told her she had a 9mm gallstone. Well, we prayed. When it was time for her surgery, they did one more check...and guess what? It was gone! They do not know what happened to it. Grandma, the outward, who talks to everyone, said, "I know what happened....Jesus Healed me... He took it!!" And she let the doctor and everyone know who healed her! In Jesus Name! Sometimes that is exactly why we go through things, because there are doctors God wants to reach and nurses etc, to show His power, to give us a testimony to share for His glory, to help others, to minister to them and be a witness.

Pap and Grandma renewing their vows

Sisters.... The first time my sister came, she was having feet trouble. She responded to come down and get prayed for. We prayed for her and as I prayed for her, I saw a five to six inch wound start to heal from the bottom up. I spoke that out. After that her feet were healed. My other sister, before she came, I saw in a vision, her coming down to the altar at my church and I saw all kinds of chains fall off of her. So, she came, it was her first time coming. She responded and came down to the front. And on the recording you can hear me praying for all the chains to be broken. For that is what I saw in my vision. Well, I did not know, I learned later that she had a neck and shoulder and back problem. She had been taking some medicine for it and had an appt. with a chiropractor. We found out later, after she wanted to make sure,....she told us she canceled her appt. and doesn't take her medicine any more; she was healed. From that service on, she had no more problems.

Dad's.... Healing, He had two herniated disks, bothering him. After prayer, and targeting his back. He was healed. There was no more problem with his back. No more pain. He was healed, In Jesus Name!

Isaiah's finger... Healed! After many years and many things trying to fix his finger. He had it smashed and an infection got in there, it was healed! And at the time of him sharing His miracle, that night before sharing, He had an awesome dream. And he shared His healing and His dream the next day! Awesome! He was eight years old.

Isaiah sharing his dream and healing testimony, age 8

"And these signs will follow those who believe: In My Name they will cast out demons; they will speak with new tongues; they will take up serpents; and if they drink anything deadly, it will by no means hurt them; they will lay hands on the sick, and they will recover." Mark 16:17-18

There were many more, many more signs and miracles.......
We ended up going over a hundred healings! Amazing for God's glory! And I realized that during this time, of our church, my kids got saved, filled with The Holy Spirit and baptized in water, Amazing!!

Hannah getting baptized

People would come and be healed, and not come back. I learned that like the ten lepers, only one came back to thank The Lord. I learned when God gave me a Word, people would have a choice. I learned by how God spoke to me, I would have many words and the ones that came received their miracles, while others,

95

that wouldn't come in God's timing, missed it. Words from The Lord of healing, words of provision, words of knowledge, prophetic words of guidance, blessings for the future, even of spouses and future mates, that were missed. Many miss their appointed times of opportunity; they miss by not obeying God at the right times, miracles and life changes in their life. And if you miss it, you miss it. Don't miss it! Pass the tests, stay in God's will and His perfect Will, will be done in your life. This is the school of God. I was shocked, many times like Naaman, (Who almost missed his healing because he didn't want to dip in the river, how and where God said.) people would miss their miracle because of pride, wanting it their way (Their church or pastor etc.) instead of humbling themselves and doing it God's way. Just like when He came the first time, how many would have missed The King of Kings, being born in the lowest of places? Only those who were to hear and humble themselves to accept God's way, would witness it. How many missed His ministry when He came passing by their area, or missed His purpose and resurrection? How many will hear The truth today? How many will accept today the way He comes? Will you miss Him because you want it a certain way, or person or place? Will you accept, where He comes and who He wants to use? In rejecting it, you are not rejecting man but God. Naaman had to dip 7 times in the river, where God said. If not, He would have missed his healing. We need many of Naaman's friends that will help get people where they need to go so they can be healed. It was the Captain of the guards, to Naaman, and his friend that said sir, if it were a hard thing would you not have done it? You see, Naaman was offended because he wanted it a certain way, a more dignified way. But his friend persuaded him to obey the prophet's words, and humble himself. He did it and was healed. We need those friends to actually help obey God's word, not the contrary. Go to their dead church? No, obey God! Naaman would have missed being healed of leprosy, because he wanted his way, a cleaner river or wanted to just have hands laid on him, etc. Well, not this time, it's God's way. God works on a higher level, even sometimes more than healing, He is working on you. (For Study: 2 Kings 5:13) He went where God said, did what God said, dipped seven times and was healed!

I was shocked by people, that would not support us or our ministry, especially when they know my life, our testimony and my little family.

Why would the church get so many others, support others with no power, not real, not Spirit, no miracles nor give altar calls? This is an amazing question I still have no answer for.

As I said before when God speaks a lot of times it is to help through the fire. WELL, THIS SAME YEAR WE TOOK A QUICK TRIP! And we did not realize how crucial & life changing it would be!!

I am so thankful for God's Word, because the devil & world & even the church a lot of times will try to make it and treat you like the opposite of who you are. His Word, through an undeniable

Man of God, was given to us, to help us maintain through the worst attacks against our family. There were three main areas of attack, My Family, Our Sports & Our Ministry. It was affecting all three areas at the same time. Affecting our dreams. I did not understand what was to come, but as God's pattern a lot of times is, He speaks a word to sustain you through the attack that will come. In connection to the attack and the level of attack, The Lord will give you that level of a Promise of God to sustain you through the attack. It just so happened I saw that Pastor Kilpatrick was having special services in Alabama with Steve Hill and Lindell Cooley. So for some reason, I knew it was crazy because it was just a weekend thing, and to go that far?!, but I wanted to go and boy am I glad we did. One of the most powerful, special words I would ever get!

(Remember, want miracles? Obey God, His way...step by faith, pay the price, risk it all & you will see the power, miracles & special things of God.)

As we were at the service, it was towards the end, Evangelist Steve Hill said if you want prayer, to come on down and get prayed for. So I definitely did. We marched our little family down to the altar and waited for prayer. We were all standing together. I was holding my daughter Rachel, in my arms, standing with my wife and kids. I will never forget. Evangelist Steve Hill, came to pray for us and what happened next changed our life. And this really is the first time, we are really sharing it. We've kept it quiet for many, many years until the proper time. It was a special powerful word, as he prayed for us He said, *"This is an Awesome family, You have an Awesome family!"*....as he prayed... (and I am not going to share everything).... There was a sign and what

98

it means.... and then he said, *"I've never done this in my 32yrs. of ministry!"* It was powerful. It was special. I couldn't believe it. And it took someone like him, A man of God, who you know is hearing from God, for me to be able to know it is completely GOD! This is the word that my family and I would constantly use, over and over in the coming days & years. Because the devil's onslaught was so great, trying to scream out over us the opposite of this Word of The Lord. But we believe God! Thank You Lord, I can not thank You enough for speaking over us and to us, a powerful, preserving word so special.

(A lot of people want a word, but will not go where and when, and with who God is using to get one. They stay in their dead religion and want God to speak, but you have to do your part, pay a price and obey God. And do whatever He wants.)

So a dream of mine, finally, after all these years, my kids are going to get to do what I could not do: (Because of my heart problem) get to play football and other competitive sports. I debated whether to wait or not, another year, because of those who cause trouble, but....We prayed about it, fasted about it, and we felt to go ahead now and play. We were excited. And Sarah, had been playing soccer, where I coached, and we had an awesome team. Also, our baseball team, went un-defeated.... Awesome, Thank The Lord. Isaiah was going to play football and Sarah said, "Well, I don't want to play soccer, I want to play football like Isaiah!" So I didn't know if she should play or not, we prayed about it...Sooo...here we came, Sarah 7 and Isaiah 6, coming to play football. (Sarah, just to let you know, was the fastest on the team... I mean, she won, every single sprint!) She took to it and Isaiah loved it. I was an assistant coach. Everyone knows we are a Christian family and that I am pastoring. Then, not long after, things started to stir. (Remember, anointed by the devil to cause me havoc.) Remember, I coached soccer a couple years before this and it went great.) So, out of the blue, pressure started happening against me and against my kids. This stirring also spread to the school, at the same time. It was Terrible. And if that wasn't enough, God kept saying something to me about Isaiah. (Remember, God said when he was born, "Don't believe anything they tell you, he's going to be everything you've wanted him to be!") Because they were mistreating him and saying all kinds of evil about this little precious boy. God kept saying to me, "They are going to let him go all year to school, and you're going to think everything is fine, and at the end, they are going to fail him and say "He failed!" So as God kept putting this on me, as the devil kept trying to ruin and mark Isaiah with lies, we inquired a little further through different means. And boy, was it exposed. It came out, that an educator at that time, went off to an inside source, spewing hatred against us, Isaiah, and even talked about my wife. We were also encouraged by those at a higher level, who saw what was happening, to pull our kids out of public school. They had seen it was ridiculous. I had already said, "That was it!" and when I heard that, about the spewing from the educator, I was done! They had brought my six and seven yr olds, secretly, into an office, without telling us, their parents or anything. They were interrogating them. BUT GOD! God gave Sarah and Isaiah, (and they didn't even know) the perfect words to say to them, the perfect responses. When I heard about this, I was done. How evil. So we were being falsely accused on every side. I had to pull my kids out of school, start homeschooling and walk away from the team because of the lies. (Which they also tried to use against my son, saying false reasons why we are homeschooling. P.S...by the way, Isaiah is a top, honor roll student and was awarded an academic & athletic scholarships for college! And Sarah also, for God's glory!) Also, at this same time, we had grown with the church and we were looking for land. We found land and were trying to buy it. The owners wanted to sell it to us, but some neighbors caused trouble. It went to court, because of the people living nearby, "Didn't want the traffic, a little church would cause....?!" (Ironically, there is now a big restaurant that sits nearby.) We ended up not being able to build. I was crushed. All my dreams, I could not understand all the evil, why would God allow this? It was tough. It doesn't really help your church and ministry to grow. Why wouldn't people want someone truly "Called", who lived for The Lord his whole life, a testimony of heart issues, childhood sicknesses, and a good family etc. Then you think as Jesus said, if they do not hear you...shake the dust off your feet. It will be more bearable for Sodom and Gomorrah on the day of judgment than for that town. (Matthew 10:14) (People and areas have choices....and consequences to those choices.) But through it all, we held on to the Promise and Word over us, "This is an Awesome Family!" and devil you can't have it. We gave it up, all of it, for The Lord. Lord's will be done. (I thought because of what I went through growing up and the denial of a lot of things, that it was going to be easy for my kids, but it was the contrary.) But thank God for His awesome word and His plan. I would not want anything else but His special plan. Like Apostle Paul said, *"By honor and dishonor, by evil report and good report; as dec*eivers, *and yet true; as unknown, and yet well known; as* *dying, and behold we live; as chastened, and yet not killed; as sorrowful, yet always rejoicing; as poor, yet making many rich; as having nothing, and yet possessing all things."* 2 Corinthians 6:8-10 (For Study: 2 Corinthians 6:4-10)

This event encouraged me, but it was still really difficult. This same year God was saying, after we had all these amazing miracles and healings, and with all that we were being accused of, The Lord said, *"They are coming for your church.... you are going to have to move."* So I said it to my family and the church. "We can't stay at this location. I don't know where we are going, but we have to go." I felt like Moses, I didn't know where we were going, but we just have to go.

How could anyone believe anything like that? A lot of times, those trying to find stuff on you, if you just look at their life, many times they try to falsely accuse you of what they are and are doing. You can see a pattern. You can see it in sports and other areas; like Politics in sports, politics in the country, in church.... everything. People do the same unfair things and use the same evil tactics. Be fair and earn it. It means nothing if you manipulate it and cheat it. And some of the worst ones you wouldn't think would do that, because they are good enough without cheating... are the worst ones, that's how they got there...but you see, it's their idol. And they have to do, anything and everything to try to get ahead. They cheat stats, lie about others, take enhancers....on & on. That's losers. Real winners, do it fair and square and give God the glory. They don't want it cheated. They are good enough and don't need to cheat. SO, don't cheat us. Be fair. It's nerdy to give into cheaters and cheat the good kid; to hold them down. No...earn it. You want it? Earn it! If you are not good enough, maybe you need to find something else. (I have seen the kids cheated in their stats, cut out of school pictures for their sports, tampered stats, lied about by parents, kids and coaches, even coaches from other teams....on & on, cheated out of awards they've earned and walk away from sports they love because of mistreatment. I have seen them surrender All to follow The Lord, even to give up friends, sports, whatever and still stand for what's right and give God The Glory! They've had to stand for Him, be an example and always in The End, because of it.... They Always come out on Top. It's a promise by God. It will always work for your good, when you stay in His will. Not so, for those who bow. I have seen them stand, in the midst of it all, not bow and God makes you the head and not the tail. And walk out with the stronghold and idols falling behind them. The enemies left with an empty idol; crumbling in their hands.)

So as we moved into the next season, as God was guiding our steps; finding and doing what we could with our kids, school & sports etc., we were also praying about a job for me. I wanted to be able to provide for my family. We had an outreach called "The Crossover", that reached many kids across multiple schools, with multiple backgrounds in our area. We would have pizza and basketball, then share the gospel and pray. Many top athletes in the area came through there. I would pick most of them up and drop them off. It went on for about 5 years. Kids responded to give their heart to The Lord. Also, fruit from it came; baptisms and even a wedding.

The Crossover

I was feeling the tug, to go outside the four walls of the church. I felt that there are so many people to reach that the church is not, that fall through the cracks. So anyway, as I became a chaplain at the hospital feeling the desire to want to reach out to the world and the unchurched. A position opened up. They wanted me to fill-in that position, for now. It was the Hospice Chaplain. So as that was going, we were praying. We continued to pray...as we were driving to minister one Sunday, Hannah at 9yrs old said, "Oh yeah, Dad....hey, I had a dream..." I said, "You did? Of what?" She said, "I saw you wearing a suit and you had in your hands "promotion." I was like, "What, are you serious?" She was dead serious. So because of that, I said, "Well, I better be wearing a suit, because of Hannah's dream." Which I did. Anyway, the position officially opened up. I applied for it. I went, wearing a suit to the interview and can you believe it....went on to get the job! What a blessing. I used to wonder what I could do that would still be ministry and still respectable. God worked it out. Amazing! I had an interview and it went really good..... I Got the job! Perfect! Such a blessing. My new title was... "Staff Chaplain-Hospice!" Hannah, some time later after this, after I got my job, reminded me of her dream, and I said, "That's right! You were right!" Don't brush kids aside, they can hear and be used by God! This was just the beginning for our family of a new season of blessings, favor, promotions, opportunities and many wonderful ministry testimonies! All for God's Glory!

Spiritual Wellness

Exploring the benefits of Hospice care at UPMC Western Maryland

There are no words to say or way to describe the moments of a family in these most critical moments. As we take the hand of the dying, both the patient and their family are trusting us to be able to give reassurance, closure and comfort.

As I take the hand of a weakening loved one, I think of Jesus' words, "I will never leave you nor forsake you." I think that we never walk alone, as Psalm 23 says. He is our Shepherd who walks with us and gives us no fear, though we walk through the valley of the shadow of death.

As we pray and give everything to Him, He promises us eternal life, and, instead of my hand, His hand takes them on to the other side, giving everyone the peace that only The Prince of Peace can give, showing and feeling God's love for the patient and each one there.

No words can say the value, meaning or reward of those moments or what it means to work with a team of unbelievable and exceptional nurses, doctors, volunteers and all who make up the interdisciplinary team.

Hospice staff members show God's love and are His hands and feet extended. They are a special breed, and I am honored to work with them and be a part of the team. The care is not just for the moment but is varying in length, distance and duration, covering mile upon mile, all kinds of terrain, and any time - day or night.

The care includes helping patients and families, making arrangements and, long afterward, offering support, follow-up calls, and grief counseling. It has also been my privilege many times to perform services, giving last words and the graveside committal.

Hopsice is an unbelievable service with immeasurable rewards. I am so thankful to be a part of it and to be able to show God's love in every situation.

The UPMC Western Maryland Hospice team is second to none and so intrinsically valuable. Their importance and value are priceless. The spiritual benefits of Hospice Care carry a lasting and eternal impact for patients, families and staff.

Thank you for letting me share these thoughts from the Hospice Chaplain's Heart.

Rev. Seth Wharton

Rev. Seth Wharton can be contacted at 240-964-8288 or by email at whartons4@upmc.edu. If interested in contacting UPMC Western Maryland Hospice, please call 240-964-9000.

Chapter 7

From Generation to Generation: Seeing The Spirit Fall On Our Kids

The Bible talks about families and the generations, and even the tribes of Israel. When Israel blessed them, he blessed them with what each tribe and family line would be. Each one according to his own blessing. (Joseph got two tribes land allotment, because of the price he paid and doing what's right. It is his two sons....Ephraim & Manasseh....He got a double portion.) Some families have different giftings. Some have Spiritual gifts of God or are used in similar giftings. Some families have giftings and mantles passed down, or other kinds of gifts and talents. The Scripture says in 2 Timothy 1:5, Paul said to Timothy, *"I am reminded of your sincere faith, which first lived in your grandmother Lois and in your mother Eunice and, I am persuaded, now lives in you also."* And as Joel 2:28 says, *"And it shall come to pass afterward that I will pour out My Spirit on all flesh; Your sons and your daughters shall prophesy,......"*

I am so thankful that my kids did not grow up in church as "usual" and in forms of godliness & denying the power. They didn't grow up in false doctrines or around the superficial but, around the Spirit, the real and seeing the miracles for themselves. Feeling God's presence, hearing & seeing the truth; It is priceless. The power of God and the truth is for everyone, unless, we put other things like self, cliques, and other things first & not want to pay a price for what's right. The price, of being lukewarm, is far worse. Proof is in the power of God. God proves His word by the accompanying signs and who He's "Called", by not talk....but power. Mark 16:20 *"And they went out and preached everywhere, The Lord working with them and confirming the word through the accompanying signs."*

I am so thankful for my wife, Kendra, like Proverbs 31. She is a good worker. She gets up early while it is still dark and takes care of her kids. She does not fear. And like 1 Peter 3:4 says, being adorned with *"the hidden person of the heart, with the incorruptible beauty of a gentle and quiet spirit, which is very precious in the sight of God."* But you will see a fierce side, if you cross a line, or attack her family. She has never had fear of man, never telling me not to say about sin or repentance or letting The Lord have His way. She has always been with me 100%, not once, has she said anything to not fan it or fearful of man to want me to compromise. She loves it. She loves when I stand, loves God having His way, loves true worship and loves to see the power of God. She loves to see true repentance, real altar calls and loves holiness. She does not need to be the center of attention, but good with being behind the scenes if need be, whatever God wants. She loves to worship. A worshiper on the piano, with her voice and with the trumpet. She truly has been given, & us put together, by God. She has had to quietly pay a price for what's right. Lied to about me & forsaking all, to do what God wanted her to do. The position of Pastor's wife, is not for the faint of heart. Give her the praise she deserves & let her kids rise up & call her blessed.

> Genesis 2:18 & 22 *"And The Lord God said, "It is not good that man should be alone; I will make him a helper comparable to him." "Then the rib which The Lord God had taken from man He made into a woman, and He brought her to the man."*

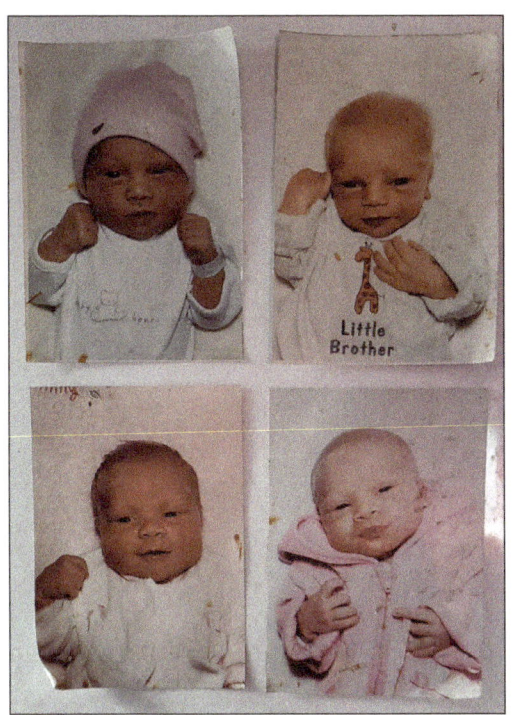

Sarah, Isaiah, Rachel, Hannah, baby photos

As we started our family....I would pray, "I don't want to have kids unless they are going to serve You!" To me it's just not worth it. And I would pray for them to be healthy & nice looking.....

blessed, gifted etc. I would bless them. (It would cross my mind because of all that I had, sickness etc., I would pray for them to be healthy.) It wasn't until Sarah Elizabeth, our first born, was born. When Kendra went into labor, I was so excited, that when I grabbed the "To Go Bag".....that as I zipped it up.... I broke the zipper right off!!

After we brought her home and as I was praying....I remember, it was out on our back deck, I was sitting and praying....that it really hit me, I started to worry, like sometimes we do.... I was praying, "Lord please, may she serve You...no sin...keep her safe..etc." I remember so clear, I felt The Lord touch me....on my head...& said, *"You are not going to have to worry about her!"* That she was going to serve The Lord. When she was four years old, God started to move in her life. We took a trip, like we like to do. We stayed in a hotel & went swimming. While we were home the next night, Sarah at 4yrs. old, started to share a dream she had, the night we were in the hotel. *She said as she dreamed, she saw Jesus, and His blood came down and covered her and Jesus came into her heart. She also said, that He was in her room, and told her, "Don't be afraid, I am taking care of you!"* Sarah had given her heart to The Lord at the age of four. We called and she shared her dream with family, it was awesome! That night while we were watching a Bible movie, Jesus showed up to the disciples in the boat, in a storm. He was walking on the water and He said, "Don't be afraid..." Sarah then said, "That's what He said to me!" Wow... I was like shocked. And said, "You're right, that's right. That's what He said to you!" And I realized, that is what He has said, a lot of times in the Bible when He would show up to people, He would say, "Don't be afraid..." Sarah was also baptized in The Holy Spirit at the age of six. Sarah is a leader. She has gifts of worship, leadership and athletic abilities. She has discernment, is doctrinally sound and is a protector of the Truth. She is our "Princess", consecrated to God," which is the meaning of her name, Sarah Elizabeth. Elizabeth after her praying great grandma. We prayed and got the kids names from The Lord. Many times in the Bible, people were given special names, as God would speak even before birth on what to name the child, the same as God would sometimes change their name. Names have meaning.

Next came what we were all praying for.....

It wasn't until about a week before, on my birthday no-less, that I got a call from Kendra. She was upset. She was just going for a baby check up. Everything had been good. She was about eight months pregnant. Normally I go with her to the appointments, but it was just to be a simple check up, so I stayed home. So, it was my birthday, all was good...then, Kendra called, crying and upset. I said, "What's wrong, what's going on?" She said, "They think there might be something wrong with the baby." I said, "Well, let's pray!" And we did.. and I was trying to tell her it will be alright. She said, "Keep praying, I will call you back." When I got off the phone, I went to The Lord, the only place you can go, the only place I knew.... I cried out to God for my SON! As I was praying and crying..and thoughts of my childhood ran through my mind...of doctors and surgeries...etc... I said, "Lord, I wanted him to be all these things..".and I went through the list...sports, and used by God, etc....but I said, "Most of all, I want him to serve You! So, not my will, but your will be done!" So I laid it all out there before The Lord. After that, I was recovering and went down in the basement, to worship. I picked up my guitar, and started to just worship the Lord. After a little bit... God touched me.... I started crying, and lifting my voice, shouting... and intercession hit me. I was really praying...and laid down on the floor...in deep prayer... and then God spoke.... He said, *"Don't believe what they tell you. Because you have given him to me, he is going to be everything you've wanted him to be. I have put my hand on him and I will not remove it!"* Wow, I was crying and thanking The Lord. How awesome, that we have a place we can turn to, that He is not a God far off but near. And if we call to Him, He will answer us. So, when Kendra called back, she was trying to tell me some things they were saying... I said, "Listen, God spoke to me, it doesn't matter what they say!" I went on to tell her the word. From then on it didn't matter. I called my parents and her parents, and with tears, told them what God had said. Up until this point we had told no one of what we were having. But as I told them... I said, " I was praying for my SON!" It was awesome and powerful. One week, exactly one week from my birthday, God gave us a Son. And I will never forget as he was being born. I saw gleaming white hair on his head, could not believe how white blonde, being born. And as he was being born, Kendra was praising God saying, "I know he's from you, he's so precious. Thank You God!!" And let me tell you, mama didn't care who heard it. She was giving God praise!

Isaiah Gabriel was born! ..... Isaiah, "Anointed by God." He is set apart. Where the devil tried to mark him with lies, even from when he was little, he is going to and already is, bringing truth. He will shame the things that are. He is anointed. A dream he had, when his finger was healed, at eight years old; was that he was lifting weights, he was trying and couldn't lift it, then he asked God, and an angel came and gave him a gift. Then he was able to lift it. His strength comes from The Lord. He was saved at four years old.. And when he was five years old, it just so happened, by The Lord, that Dad and I were just talking about how I was Isaiah's age when I got filled with The Holy Spirit. That night during our family devotions before bed, while Isaiah was praying, lying on the floor in our living room, when He was finished praying..... He just started speaking in Tongues. He was baptized in The Holy Spirit just lying there on our floor. With no one laying their hands on him, just him praying. And it was like a sign to me, that me and Dad just talked about it that day. Awesome! When Isaiah's ministry started, it was in a unique way. We were going to surprise everyone at our next Sunday ministering at the nursing home. So he was secretly praying and preparing, we didn't tell anyone else. Little did I know, that was crucial because, I happened to get called to the hospital and I could not be there, so he had to fill in. It was a divine appointment because I would've been stuck. God worked it out. I couldn't get there and he was already prepared to minister and it was awesome. It was another sign of God's hand at starting his ministry. I was told, at the end of his preaching, the people started clapping. It was awesome, they loved him and God worked it out. He has a special gift of strength that comes from The Lord when he asks Him. He can run and he's a very good runner. He is fearless in any endeavor, football and any sport. He is one that will run in such a way as to win the prize. He is one that God uses to shame the things that are, don't count him out because he will come back to shame you. Do not touch him, God's anointed. God is with him.

He is anointed. God's got His hand on him and will not remove it. He is everything I've wanted him to be. Isaiah Gabriel....means "God is Salvation, Messenger!"

Next, Rachel Dawn......I was praying about her name. Rachel, because of being beautiful in the Bible, and she was the one that was loved. And I was wondering about Dawn, is it in the Bible? As I was praying about it, I turned right to where it says "At Dawn" they went to the tomb! So, I knew that was her name. Rachel Dawn means "Little lamb, in the morning." I felt she has a unique sound, and that while Kendra was giving birth, she was worshiping and singing, with unique beautiful sounds, groanings of beautiful worship. Rachel has many different gifts. She is very unique. From cooking, sewing, acting, video editing, a unique voice in worship, different instruments, sports, our only left-hander, many different giftings and a personality to win people over. People are just attracted to her. Even at a young age of two & three, she would just make worshipful sounds, and be singing, and a merry heart throughout the day. At 3 yrs old, she came down to the altar at our church while I was ministering on her own to get prayed for and starting speaking in tongues. It was so awesome! She had given her heart to The Lord and was filled with The Holy Spirit. I picked her up in my arms and was walking around the altar saying, "The Lord just filled my little girl with The Holy Spirit."

Hannah Faith.....so fitting... Our fourth child and the baby. Before she was born, before we knew anything. I felt The Lord speak to me and I shared with the church that "Unexpected Blessings are on the way!" Right after that, like the next day.... and we were not expecting anything.... Kendra found out she was pregnant! She is our "Unexpected Blessing" Wow!! Kendra, while pregnant, was praying for a girl with curly blonde hair & blue eyes. Well, she got her prayer answered, a naturally curly blonde haired, blue-eyed....girl. Who, also, was the only one to say "Mom" first. She has shown that once she gets a prayer request, she continues to pray until it breaks through. She is our little intercessor. Even from the time she was little, she would pray until it breaks through. If we would forget, she would bring up the prayer request and stay on it. A true intercessor. (One time, a worker friend of Mom's was in need of prayer and specifically asked for her to tell Hannah. People had already started to see the special answers to her prayers and FAITH she has. Do you know what?... Her friend got an answer to her prayer! If you need something broke through, a praying friend, someone that will fan and spread FAITH, Hannah is the one to ask for.) At the Father's day dinner our church had, when she was 3yrs old, she received the baptism of The Holy Spirit, with the evidence of speaking in tongues, when she came forward and had hands laid on her. It was just our little family praying with her on Father's day. It was special. Then, also when she was 5yrs old, on Fathers day, she was baptized in water. (It is an Outward sign of an inward cleansing... and God commanded it...so, get baptized if you haven't! Scripture says, "Repent and be baptized....") Hannah Faith means... "Favor, Grace and complete trust in God." She has a prophetic gift, which at a young age, was already activated. She spoke things she saw, (vision) and in dreams also. Things that were prophetic and they came about. She is sincere, and one that will win. Hannah laughs at her enemies. She will see it broken through and come about. She has a gift of the Spirit of Faith. She will bring the Faith for a miracle and the breakthrough for answered prayer you need. In everything, she is an Overcomer! She will Overcome.

(A "Precious" Word, just like their mother. One day while working, Kendra received a special word from a lady she was taking care of. Out of the blue the older lady gave her a word, she said, "God spoke to me and gave me a word for you, He said that He was going to give you "Precious In-laws." I probably will not be around to see it, but that is what I felt as I was praying for you." Kendra was surprised. It was from a special sweet lady. And to remember, just like her, when she was praying about coming down to school with me or not, that is what God spoke to Her. That she is "Precious." And God worked it out for us, and God will work it out in the future.... for each one who follows The Lord. Only The Lord can make it "Precious.")

All different & special, That's Our Lord. Always moving in fresh, new, special ways...infinitely unique...that's Our Lord. Special to each one and each one special to The Lord. For the ones who are willing to pay the Price & answer The High "Calling" of God, He will bless to a Thousand Generations to those who love Him....but curses to the third & fourth generation of those who do not serve Him.....SO, as Joshua says....I say over My Family & future line as long as The Lord tarries..... "As for me & my house...We will serve The Lord!"

Choose you this day whom you will serve...God is no respecter of persons. If you want the special of God, serve Him, forsaking all others. The Bible says, "Today is the day of salvation!" So don't wait. You may never get another chance. God loves you & has a plan for your life. His grace is sufficient. If you have things in your life...sin, anything that grieves The Lord, Get it right today. He will forgive. He will set free. If you want to make sure, if you want to know Him and for Heaven to be your home one day, to be saved and born again, if you're not where you should be with Him, if you want "The special plan" God has for your life... where there is the supernatural, miracles & signs of God...where you don't have to go it alone..... Pray with me right Now..... "Lord, I come to you a sinner....I ask You now, today.....Please, forgive all my sins....anything I have done to grieve You....anything I have done to hurt others..... and myself.....please forgive me...set me completely free....come into my heart...I give you my life completely...come...live Your life through me...Thank You Lord....In Jesus Name...Amen."

Now if you have prayed that, you are forgiven...born again! Heaven is rejoicing. Welcome to your New walk with The Lord. (2 Corinthians 5:17, Romans 10:9-10, John 3:3 & 3:16, 1 John 1:9) Now, some things to do as you Grow. Find a True Spirit-led church, where they preach about sin, give altar calls for people to get saved & have the power of God. Seek to be filled, receive the Baptism of The Holy Spirit with evidence of speaking in Tongues. It's power to live right, witness, is a prayer language & opens you up to the power & gifts of The Holy Spirit. We love you and God loves you. Let us know what God is doing in your life and how this book has blessed you.

Contact us at:
Rev. Seth G. Wharton
Email: swmi@atlanticbb.net
Phone: 301-707-1836
Facebook: Like & Follow us at Seth Wharton Ministries Inc.

We look forward to hearing from you! I also encourage you to Get Our 1st book "Our Hearts Desire is Our littlest Miracle" Part II. My Mom shares her heart and is an anointed writer! It will really bless you and is a testimony of God bringing us through sickness & other things, miracles, that will bless & encourage you & others. We have seen & encourage, passing it around! Pass the books around once you've read it and let us know the stories and testimonies from them. It is such a help to those going through the fire!

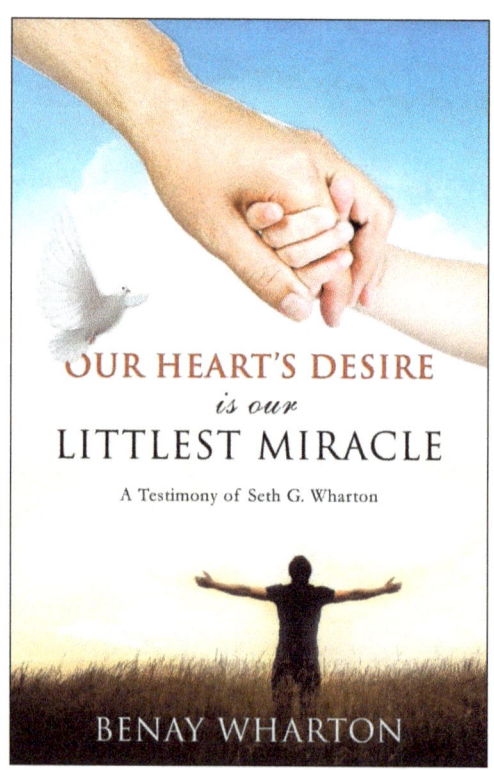

Conclusion

Remember, This is my testimony. And we overcome by The Blood of The Lamb and by the word of our testimony!! I had to share it, you share it and you have to share yours! The best testimony is the one who has stayed with The Lord, their whole life. Pass it on. It's how we Overcome! In Jesus Name!! Amen.

God bless you and thank you for letting us share our heart and testimony with you. The testimony goes on.....

The Next Chapter Is Now Being Written.......

Sarah and Isaiah "Spirit Week"

Sarah & Isaiah receiving sports awards

Rachel's Basketball

Our family leading worship for thanksgiving at the hospital.

Hannah catching the ball in the All-Star game

A Sign God is with Isaiah (Kendra sent me this picture about a minute after me praying for God to show He is with us)

Christmas Eve pictures, pyramids & Pajamas tradition

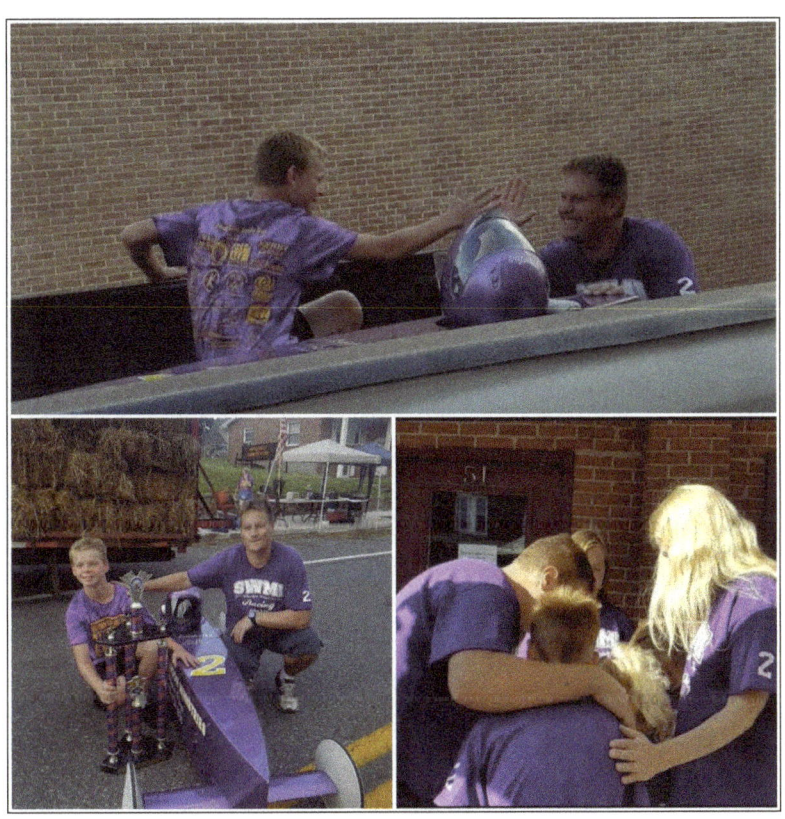

Isaiah winning 1ˢᵗ place, Frostburg Derby Day age 12

Like father, like son at Frostburg Elks Derby Day

An 'Awesome' finish as Isaiah Wharton drives to victory in same car dad used in 1990

HEATHER B. WOLFORD
HWOLFORD@TIMES-NEWS.COM

FROSTBURG — Twelve-year-old Isaiah Wharton won first place at the 41st Frostburg Elks Derby Day race on Tuesday driving the same car his father used to snag the title nearly two decades earlier.

"I thank the Lord that I got first place," Isaiah Wharton said.

Seth Wharton, 1990 Derby Day champion and Isaiah's father, said the family couldn't believe the win.

"We can't believe he won," Seth Wharton said.

"It's amazing," he said. "We are so thankful."

At least three generations of Wharton's cheered as Isaiah drove "Awesome" — a purple car featuring his dad's ministry decal — down Main Street on the Fourth of July. Benay

SEE LIKE — 3A

Ken Nolan/Times-News

Isaiah Wharton won first place in the Frostburg Elks Derby Day race on Tuesday driving the same car his father won the title in nearly two decades earlier.

Like: Father-son take titles at Derby Day

CONTINUED FROM 1A

Wharton, Seth's mom and Isaiah's grandmother, said the day brought back memories.

"When (Seth) won this race in 1990, it was such an encouragement to all of us," Benay Wharton said, "because of all he was going through."

Born with a heart defect, Seth Wharton had two open heart surgeries by age 12. He was set to have his third following his 1990 win.

"(Seth) was going through so many things at that time," she said, "and to win that race was amazing."

Now happily married with four children and head of Seth Wharton Ministries Inc., he defied the odds.

"I never thought I'd see (Seth's) son in the same car years later," Benay Wharton said. "It means so much to Seth and Isaiah."

The annual Derby Day race was founded in 1977 by the Frostburg Elks Lodge as a centennial gift to the community and a way to maintain family values, officials said.

"The idea was to bring back morals that seemed to be slipping away from American life," Dale Iman, exalted ruler of Frostburg Elks Lodge 470, said.

"The founding fathers of this event envisioned fathers and sons working together and building their cars, racing them and going through the trials and tribulations of winning and losing," Iman said.

The night before the race, Mom had a word that The Lord was going to be with him tomorrow. Seth's prayer leading up to this, because Isaiah is running out of time, Prayed and vowed Lord if You let him win tomorrow, he will be done racing

and that is what happened, he walked away a winner

Hannah, Isaiah & Me racing and winning 1st place in the same derby car, The only time that has happened for a Father and Son, let alone a Daughter also.

My blessing over the Hope and Healing Center for UPMC Western Maryland

Sarah as a freshman leading prayer before a varsity city game

Rachel in a play

Rachel & Hannah

Rachel & Hannah's softball, age 10 & 7

Kendra leading worship

God divinely working out the start of Isaiah's preaching

After walking away in 10th grade, from basketball, her dream, for The Lord; the next year with a new coach, after persecution, came back to play ending up being the leading scorer, leading rebounder and the team having the best season in 20yrs, she was also awarded MVP

Isaiah playing football, basketball & running track

Rachel playing basketball, volleyball & softball

Hannah playing basketball and running in a 5k

Senior pics & school pics

Kendra and I

Our Christmas Day Miracle

THE MIRACLE LIFE OF CHRISTMAS

I am so thankful for Christmas and life. I love this time of year, spending time with those we love and celebrating Christmas. Also, of course, all the food and presents! The Christmas life and all its meaning get more valuable to me as the years go on. You see, it's a miracle I am even here. Last Christmas, the story of my life broke on Christmas Day! You see, I was born with a heart problem; a pin-sized hole kept my little body alive. My parents did all they knew; they turned and cried out to God to spare my life. They also got as many churches and people to pray as they could. God had mercy on me. My first open heart surgery was when I was only one month old; rarely done in the world then. I ended up having three open heart surgeries, six cardiac catheterizations, five blood clots, a deadly disease called S.B.E subacute bacterial endocarditis and two valves replaced simultaneously. It was a very long and extensive surgery for only thirteen years old.

During these times, time and time again, God intervened miraculously in my life. A scripture I loved when I was 11 years old and going through my deadly disease was Psalms 91. Part of it says, "He who dwells in the secret place of the Most High shall abide under the shadow of The Almighty,"..vs. 15 "He shall call upon Me, and I will answer him; I will be with him in trouble; I will deliver him and honor him. With long life I will satisfy him and show him my salvation." All this is chronicled in my mom's published book. This year, my story has spread throughout the country and worldwide and translated into different languages.

I became the longest survivor of a double heart valve replacement, and I am in the Guinness Book of World Records, 2023 edition, on page 72. My heart is encouraging as many people as possible to help bear their burdens. No matter how bad things may look, all things are possible. To be with them, encourage and pray for them. To know through it all, God is good. I am living proof that God answers prayer. I am thankful to so many for their prayers, for doctors, for family and all the support. I was told I could not do so many things, but God had other plans that defied the odds. When people know my story and are sick, going to have surgery or have had surgery, there is an instant connection beyond words. I am willing to share my story with whoever would want to hear it. You see, I have so much more to be thankful for; he saved my life physically and spiritually. And as long as I live, may my heartbeat tell of God's saving grace for this life and the life to come. For the hope, we have in Christ. The reason for Him to come as a baby in a manger and go to the cross was His heart beating for you, for me, for all who would accept Him. He is all love. Nothing like knowing Jesus and having a personal relationship with Him for Christmas. To pray and accept His love and sacrifice for you. He loves, He forgives, and He wants you to come. Just pray now; he will hear and love you! May God bless you and your family. May you have a wonderful holiday season and a blessed New Year! I bless you with God's love, health and peace. I bless the New Year to be full of Joy! I bless you with the miracle life of Christmas!

Merry Christmas!

Thanks for letting me share the Hospice Chaplain's miracle, saved heart!

Rev. Seth Wharton

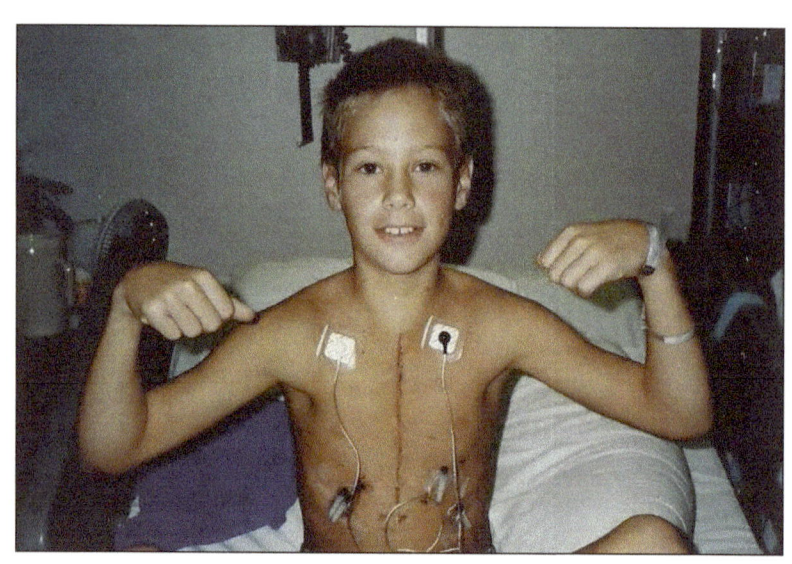

Section II: A Little Bit More

Then Came Seth

A journey of mercy, grace, sacrifices, miracles and successes as seen through Parent's eyes. Pain comes in many forms, physical, emotional, mental, regrets, fear, the feeling that you are alone in your pain and suffering. The fear of losing all you have invested and gained through dishonesty and jealousy. I have seen this firsthand when the support group you assumed would always be there for you faded away and was not. And you ask, what happened and Why?

Well, let me start by saying…Bob and I started our marriage and home out as Christians. We had been married 10 years and God had blessed us with 3 children. We had a nice home and very little problems. Life was good. I would tell everyone with a problem, "Just pray about it and God will answer." I still believe that, But…**Then came Seth…**

I tell him, "Life was easy and simple till you came along." Well I was with our 4th child and everyone in the family was praying for a boy. We had 2 girls and 1 boy and now wanted another boy. Our prayers were answered…Seth was born. The Lord even gave Bob his name; he was to be named, **"Seth Gabriel Wharton."** Later we found out that Seth means "Appointed" & Gabriel means "Messenger". God gave us **"Our Heart's Desire"** and soon we would learn that he would also become **"Our Little Miracle."**

When Seth was born, Bob was thrilled with the fact that he had the biggest chest in the nursery and we were proud…but later found out why? Seth had a heart murmur and was diagnosed with severe Aortic Stenosis, which was a narrowing of the Aortic valve. At one month of age he was then scheduled for his first of three Open Heart Surgeries. The night before surgery Bob asked the Doctor, if he was going to examine Seth one more time to be sure he still had a problem. Bob wanted to be sure he still really needed the surgery because Bob had been praying and expecting a miracle. Well Seth also had a rash all week and we were treating it with a prescription medication and had tried everything to get rid of it. It was stubborn and was still there the night before surgery. Bob prayed, "Lord help us to know your hand is on Seth and take his rash away. And Lord please help him not to be upset in the morning from his pre-surgery shots; in fact let him sleep through it all, Please."

The next day, the day of surgery, when we arrived at the hospital, we laid our hands on Seth and began to pray. Bob looked at me and said, "Do you notice anything Benay, "Yes the rash is gone, all gone." That was the sign Bob had prayed, that God was with us. The nurse came and gave him his shots, he cried furiously for a few seconds and then went right back to sleep and slept clear through the whole thing. "Jesus He is yours," as we watched his bed disappear down the hall for surgery. This was the beginning of my prayer list, that became a book, **"Our Heart's Desire is Our Littlest Miracle."** What started out as a prayer list ended up as a book of miracles. I had a notebook and I would write the things we needed to target for prayer, and then call my Mom back home, who would then call the prayer requests to others. And so it was… I began to notice that the prayers I had prayed several days before had been answered…WOW. It's funny how we ask, expect and then miss the very answers to our prayers. This was the beginning of a journey of learning to Trust the Lord and lean not to our own understanding. (Proverbs 3:5 & 6.) That also in every situation to look for the blessing. You may not always see it at first, but it's there and in time you will see it.

Well the doctors and heart specialists said Seth would never be able to run a mile, play competitive sports or work construction, which was pretty much the definition of our family. But they said, he would otherwise have a chance for a normal life. In the Wharton home that was a normal life. It seemed Ironic that the very things Seth would not be able to do (according to the doctors) were the main things our family did…Construction and Sports. But God had different plans. Seth did run a mile and more, he did work construction & on & on things God did, doctors said would not happen and now runs in 5K's with his family. Look what the Lord has done!!!! There was a girl healed of Cancer, one time and she would tell her testimony everywhere and every chance she would get and she said, "I know people get tired of me giving my testimony, but I will never get tired of telling it and what the Lord has done." And that is how I feel. I will NEVER get tired of telling it, because it never gets old as to what God has done and is doing.

It's hard to believe that Seth is now a Hospice Chaplain, for the Hospital. And thinking back so many years ago when he was born the youngest of 4. Seth's journey from the time of his birth has been an amazing miracle. As parents, we have lived Seth's life with him. From surgery to surgery, Cardiac Catheterizations, Digoxin and Lasix when he was in Congestive Heart Failure as a baby, to Coumadin as a teen and for life. The time the Dr. told Bob and me, we would know in the morning if Seth would be ok. That night I cried and Bob prayed all night. The physical limitation that the doctors put on Seth and said he would never be able to play competitive sports, run a mile, lift weights or work construction with his Dad, which I confess was what our family was all about... God, Family, Sports and Construction. Yep that was it. We watched him as he'd play in the yard with friends and his physical ability was amazing and far above normal, yet couldn't play for his school like his siblings and friends had done. Did it stop him? No. I guess he was Dr. Brenner's, Cardiologist at JHH, worst nightmare and yet also his hero. When Seth would have his Cardiology visit, Dr. Brenner would bring a medical student in to meet Seth and ask him, "Well Seth what are you benching now?" On one of the last visits with Seth now in his 20's He said, "I have to admit and tell you, you have taught me a lot. We learn from our patients too." Dr. Brenner showed his pride in Seth's never quit, defying the odds attitude. Dr. Brenner even got Seth and Kendra a wedding present. Wow, the medical and physical issues were hard, yet he faced them head on. During a Men's BB championship, Seth twisted his ankle, it swelled extra because of his coumadin, we pray & then Go! The guys wrapped it in duct tape and he played to help win the opportunity for the championship game, and then went to the hospital. Needless to say the

ED Doctor was overwhelmed and distraught, but Seth said, "It was worth it."

Yes he did run a mile and more, and competed in bench press meets and won his age bracket and worked construction with his Dad. (See our 1st book of testimony) He played on 3 youth Basketball teams his senior year in high school. He also won The Dapper Dan Most Courageous Athlete Award when he was 14. Then went on to play college Basketball at Southeastern Bible School and received his Black Belt in Karate. He has led a life of many disappointments, and sacrifices but has overcome with victories and successes that only comes from his faith and trust in God. In which is why these books of testimony are so powerful and necessary. He has overcome by the blood of the Lamb and the word of his testimony. One of the most disappointing of times for Seth, was when family support that had always been there at all times, faded away and Seth's heart was disappointed as was mine. I don't think kids and Seth ever know the agony and heartaches, the sleepless nights parents have and thousands of prayers prayed. Parents that live and struggle with him, in every disappointment, surgery, and yes celebrate all the victories and wins too.

Seth never looked sick, and that got him into trouble. It was his senior year of high school that he began to get such a hunger for God and prayer. Although he had always prayed and read his Bible, now at age 16 he couldn't get enough of God and Prayer. At camp he was a counselor and he prayed with his boys and almost all were filled with the Spirit. In his Sunday School class, kids were getting saved and filled, then Seth and the Youth went to the Revival. Well he came back from the Revival with a greater hunger and a greater move of God's Spirit in his life. He would be up praying and worshiping till 1-2 am in the morning. I would get up to go to the bathroom and I would hear him praying. We didn't understand completely all that was going on spiritually. We just didn't. (We were concerned that we were becoming like Job's comforters.) We reasoned it out and yes we always prayed, but I remember saying, "You're not getting enough sleep, or too much prayer, or you've had too much revival, you need balance." We didn't know that Seth was in God's training camp of, "The Called", that only Seth and God could understand. We didn't see the battle Seth was going through of seeing the price he would have to pay to do God's will. We prayed, pleaded the blood over Seth, we took authority over the devil and we even tried the "Will Thing", like, "You don't have to be in this thing." Boy that was a big help or "Stand against this attack". It was like telling him, to not obey God, come off the cross & it will be easier. Now that was spiritually wise and encouraging words. But in it all it seemed like everything Seth's hands would touch, God would bless but boy would it come with attack.

Bob, his father's take on Seth's life says, "Seth was always tuned in with the Lord. He always went the extra with the Lord. Seth prayed about everything as a boy and now as a Father himself, a Hospice Chaplain and Pastoral Care Chaplain. Seth's fellowship with the Lord is prayer and The Lord is always first. As a kid, we would see him turn his face always away from anything bad. He is tuned in with the Lord morning, noon and night. I can expect a word or message sent through to my phone at any time day or night and I look forward to it. Seth keeps me on my toes. Seth has always went through his problems stoically and with faith in the Lord. The things Seth would do in the church would stand out.

One time he was asked to play a violin in the church Play and it stood out…spiritually and was anointed and to me was the biggest part of the play. Seth always stood for what was right all through school and was always a good example. All the kids wanted to be around him. Seth now has a family of his own and if you had to pick a family, you would put his family as the highest. His kids are all obedient and all serve the Lord and are all really outstanding. If you graded Seth he would be #1 in performance and spiritually outstanding. His kids are all healthy and even his kids would be rated #1. Seth was 100% out of everything he did, even with his problems... Seth had a lot of problems that no normal person had to go through and he always made the best of every problem. I remember the Lord would talk to him on his little motorcycle. This was the cycle I got him as a prize for going through his 2nd Open Heart Surgery at age 5. But Seth and his cycle was also spiritual. Seth was a standout in whatever he did. Today he is still a standout in everything he and his family do. Seth is the Hospice and Pastoral Chaplain at the hospital and is right where God wants him. He has great opportunities to minister to people and this is made just for him and this is just the beginning."

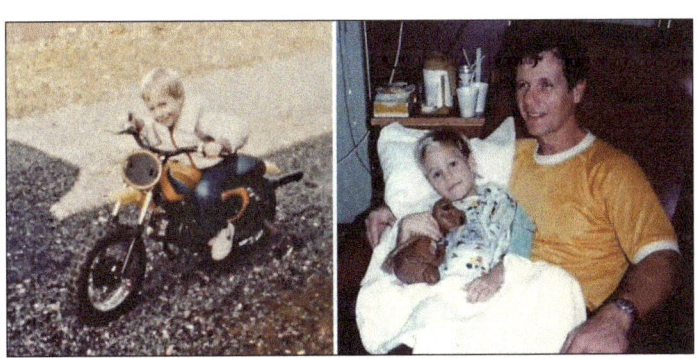

Seth riding his motorcycle and sitting with his Dad age 5

The call of God to ministry on your life takes on a whole new meaning when you answer, "The Call" and give all. I am talking about a call from God, not from your parents or those who might encourage you to go into ministry because you have talents of speaking or singing or more, but the real call of God that requires you give all. Take up HIS CROSS and follow HIM at any price. The true "Call" from God may be different & is different from what you think. It is confirmed by God. And listen to them, though you don't understand, listen & be there for them. For being "Called" of God is truly a high price, that a lot you can not see and is more than the average Christian. Those "Called" have a greater price & responsibility. Give them the honor due to them who have been proven & walk faithfully. The price of the cross is worth it, in the end a blessing, powerful, real and glorifying to The Lord. The greater the "Call", the greater the price.

I end with my poem of Seth's Call:

The Call

Many are called by peers, family, and friends
For talents and orator skills they possess
But the one on one call of the Lord
Leads to a prepared Desert experience

The call to ministry for God's perfect plan
Requires surrender and sacrifice
To be ready to give ALL in His name
And to pay "the cost" at any Price

From the time you were just a baby
He held you close in heartache and strife
He spared your life time after time
God worked miracles in your life

In Chemistry class you surrendered
To the will and call of the Lord
Knowing the price you'd have to pay
Yet a call that could not be ignored

Appointed a herald, apostle, teacher
Preaching Jesus is what you love most
The little boy with heart problems
Has been called to a prophet's post

You have been entrusted with a ministry
The powerful anointing no one mistakes
A healing ministry of many healings
That now reaches over many states

The little boy hindered in playing sports
Spending time in hospitals as a boy
Now has the hand of God on his shoulder
And the Father's bounty to enjoy

God Bless You Seth, we love you
And are proud and stand in Awe
As the glorious Blessings are given
And the Lord reveals to you, His all

Words, Prophesies, visions and Dreams
The Lion of Judah, the living seal
As the Lord's Mysteries unfold
Your future will be powerfully revealed

Who can stand against the Lord's anointed?
What obstacle can stand in God's way?
Everything He has promised, He will do!
He's the great "I Am" every single day

As you walk humbly before the Lord
May your relationship grow in every way
Feasting in His Glorious Blessings
With your Calling renewed every day

As Seth says, "All for God's Glory"

Our first published book

Mom & Dad & Seth

Me & my Dad

Section III

The Baptism of The Holy Spirit: "Receiving, Praying & Using"

*A*postle Paul said, *"I Thank my God I speak with tongues more than you all......"* 1 Corinthians 14:18 and he was used to write most of the New Testament.

> Acts 2:38-39 *"Then Peter said to them, "Repent, and let every one of you be baptized in the name of Jesus Christ for the remission of sins, and you shall receive the gift of The Holy Spirit. For this promise is to you and to your children, and to all who are afar off, as many as The Lord our God will call."*

The gift of The Holy Spirit is for everyone....for *ALL* whom The Lord our God will call!

The Spirit is the Power....& if it's God, I want it! I want all God has for me.... and to not want Him, is wrong....to reject The Spirit &/or gifts of The Holy Spirit .. ....you are rejecting God Himself.

Jesus said, "It is better I go away so that The Comforter will come....." & Greater works will you do, because He goes to The Father...

Jesus also said, "Out of your belly will flow rivers of living waters, by this He meant The Spirit"...(John 7:37-39) and "Your body is the temple of The Holy Spirit" (1 Corinthians 6:19)

Your body can be filled with The Holy Spirit... I have experienced this personally, with The Holy Spirit.....like a river, flowing out of me...and words, as the Spirit gave the utterance. And also used in gifts of The Holy Spirit.

A main thing missing in these last days.... Is The baptism of The Holy Spirit. Even many "Pentecostal" churches do not emphasize... the Baptism. Without The Spirit filled & Spirit led ministry... all you have left is a form of Godliness & denying the POWER... of which the Bible says, "Have nothing to do with them." How can we accept "ministries" without supernatural Power? It's not ministry.....it's "Flesh-istry."

No power for miracles, No power to live right, no power or conviction of The Holy Spirit, which draws & leads to salvation.... we must be "Born Again" of The Spirit...drawn by The Spirit...not flesh converts....They are not "Born Again." (*"Woe to you scribes and Pharisees, hypocrites! For you travel land and sea to win one proselyte, and when he is won, you make him twice as much a son of hell as yourselves."* Matthew 23:15)

No real ministry without The Holy Spirit....& He can not be manipulated!!

The reason why people can not receive, get offended or understand the things of The Spirit is because they do not have The Spirit. They can not in the flesh grasp the ways of God. Some have been wrongfully taught, some want their own way, and still some because of seeing the fake, (which is understandable) have been turned off,...but the real is still true! Throw out the fake, and don't let the "fakers" cause you to grieve and miss The Holy Spirit, what God wants to give to you, to bless and help you. For <u>All</u> God has for you. (For Study: 1 Corinthians 2:14, Matthew 11:25)

I received The Baptism of The Holy Spirit at 5 years old.... a day before my 2nd open heart surgery... it was strength & encouragement, and to show God was with us... He gave me a prayer language and to my family it was a sign that God was with us!

Not long after that.... God spoke to me....

While riding my little motorcycle.... Awesome! (See Part II of "Our Heart's Desire is Our Littlest Miracle.")

The Baptism opens you up to The Spirit....His Gifts, how He moves....To be used in Power...not flesh and dead, a grinding, but Spirit & life. It also helps you in understanding how He speaks spiritually & To know His voice... Without The Spirit & in the flesh; The Spirit looks like foolishness, but when you have The Holy Spirit, you start to understand His ways & why. In your own knowledge you miss The Power & Spirit of God.

The Main reasons to be filled.....Jesus said, "Go and wait, for to be clothed with Power from on High." (Luke 24:49, Acts 1:4-8 & Acts 2:1-4) Then, "Go into all the world"....(Mark 16:15-20) Many want to skip the waiting & empowerment...and just "Go".... but don't Go without first being clothed with power...it's power to witness, power to minister...fire...to be truly on fire & for God's Glory, to go where and when He wants you, (If you don't wait... You're on your own...All flesh..) fire to burn out the flesh.... Flesh and Spirit are at odds with each other. So unless you are clothed with Power and unless you are led by The Holy Spirit, then all you do will actually be against God, and stealing from what God wants to do. No matter what it is, good works, ministry etc. will take away and actually be against The Lord, and does nothing for God's Kingdom. We must be Spirit filled and Led, then it's for His Glory & true ministry. Without the Cross there is no Spirit, without the flesh being crucified there is no Power. Man's wisdom +Self Glory = no power.

(Flesh is so tempting, you get it easy, get praise from men, but in the end is death. And the Cross can hurt, when flesh is spiteful, but in the end you have life & the real, that is pleasing to The Lord, glorifying to Him... what's of The Spirit & lasting.... not empty flesh & death. If your heart truly wants the truth and God's way, you'll accept the cross and The Spirit. You will not accept the flesh.)

Jesus said, "It's a gift...." just receive this gift... John the Baptist said, "I indeed baptize you.... but one coming after me that will baptize you in The Holy Spirit & with fire." John's was a Baptism of repentance in water, Jesus' Baptism is in The Holy Spirit & fire for every believer.

And if Jesus wants you to have this gift from Him, shouldn't you want it too? Don't let the devil, pride or anything else keep you from receiving this wonderful gift, that everyone can have.....

To clear some things up....

Two Different Tongues.... One is a <u>Baptism</u>, a prayer language for every believer...to empower you and open you up to spiritual gifts.

<u>The second</u>: is one of the nine gifts of The Holy Spirit. In which the gifts of The Holy Spirit are: wisdom, word of knowledge, faith,

healings, miracles, prophecy, discerning of spirits, different kinds of tongues and interpretation of tongues..(I Corinthians 12:4-11).... The Spirit determines who gets what gift of The Spirit... And that is where there is a message given in tongues to the church... and these messages in tongues, must be interpreted by someone who has the gift of interpretation. Both are gifts. But the baptism, every believer can have...whereas, the gifts of The Spirit are given as the Spirit determines. So one is a Gift of The Holy Spirit, where the other is the Baptism that every believer can have, and Jesus is The Baptizer in The Holy Spirit where as the gifts are distributed as the Spirit wills. You cannot pick which gift you want, that is determined by The Holy Spirit, but the Baptism is for every believer with the evidence of speaking in tongues, a prayer language and power for ministry and to witness and to open you up to the gifts of The Holy Spirit. (For Study: 1 John 4:1, Galatians 5: 16-25, Hebrews 5:12-14)

Groans that cannot be uttered....

> Romans 8:26, *"Likewise the Spirit also helps in our weaknesses. For we do not know what we should pray for as we ought, but the Spirit Himself makes intercession for us with groanings which cannot be uttered."*

There is a Higher prayer....Higher than just words...there are cries....there are groans.... intercession....groanings of intercession by The Spirit....flowing out of you....that words cannot express.

I have seen & felt it powerfully myself. I have seen it unlock great miracles.... Turnarounds... Salvations. Let The Spirit intercede through you & out of you.

When you don't know how or what to pray....(Roman 8:26) you can pray in tongues...in the Spirit.... & it's the perfect prayer... praying according to the will of God.... Scripture says, "I will pray with the Spirit, and also pray with the understanding...." God's ways are higher than our ways...Pride & fleshly things will keep you from the things of God... being used to your fullest and help others for His Kingdom. "He keeps it from the wise & learned... but reveals it to babes...." And some can not receive because spiritually discerned..... If you are on your own, with wrong motives you will never get or understand the ways of The Holy Spirit, but if you come as a little child, God will reveal to you His Kingdom, and it will make perfect sense why He does things the way He does it....so that no flesh will Glory in His presence. He alone is worthy to be glorified, He alone can save....

Just receive....you'll be so glad you did....

(For Study: Romans 8, Ephesians 6:18, Jude 1:20-24, John 14:12-17, John 14:23-26)

To Receive: I have seen many, many receive the Baptism of The Holy Spirit...

First, make sure you are clean & right with The Lord....repent of anything unclean or anything, that's sin, that would grieve The Lord.....(go ahead and do that now) Just ask The Lord to forgive you, and give everything to Him. Tell Him you want All He has for you. If it's Him, you want it...

My Dad received the baptism of The Holy Spirit at home by himself....praying in his chair for me, while I was having a

Cardiac Catheterization....after seeking The Lord for years about it..... He just all the sudden was praying in tongues before he knew what happened, he could feel The Holy Spirit talking in him...he said he could feel there is just an unending language...

Some receive right away...while others take longer... I don't understand why it's different, but it's all special, and I think sometimes God wants people to seek Him more....The promise is for everyone! How much more will He give The Holy Spirit to those who ask Him! Jesus said, *"If you being evil, know how to give good gifts to your children, how much more will Your Heavenly Father give The Holy Spirit to those who ask Him!"* Luke 11:13. So Ask Him!!

I have seen little kids receive....& adults.....at homes, hotels, churches...and on & on....it doesn't matter where you're at.... by yourself or someone praying for you....just hunger & thirst....surrender all & you will be filled.... *"Blessed are those who hunger & thirst for righteousness, for they shall be filled!"* Matthew 5:6

Pray & ask Him....(do it now) Then step out in faith.....speak, as the Spirit gives the utterance.....

Not someone teaching you words...that's flesh.....& wrong..... The Spirit....Jesus...is The Baptizer.....The Spirit will give you the utterance, the language...as you step out in faith..... Take time right Now, seek & ask; receive. Step in faith & be filled with The Holy Spirit. It will change your life & ministry.

To Grow in: for the babes as well as mature

Just like anything else....if you don't use it....you lose it. If you use it...it will grow....use it! The Spirit of God is crying out for Him, to be allowed to use God's people to intercede.... to see great miracles....healings and people saved! For the Kingdom of

God....The Spirit intercedes, Jesus lives to make intercession for you, the Bible says for us to make intercession....

Will you let Him use you?

It will not happen without The Spirit,...souls, miracles...everything....will not happen without The Spirit, without intercession.

If you are ashamed of Him, He will be ashamed of you! And like a fire, if you fan it...it will spread!! (Are you ashamed of how He moves? How He comes?)

Bible says, "Do not quench The Spirit...

Do not grieve The Spirit...

and Do not forbid speaking in tongues!"

Blaspheming The Holy Spirit....is the only sin you cannot be forgiven of...

do not touch or speak against Him...

Test everything....throw out the fake & flesh....but do not grieve what is truly God, do not reject God....receive it...fan it.... Don't end up with just a "form of godliness"....and you denying the Power....which is the moving, in ALL His ways...of The Holy Spirit.... (while writing this...I felt The Holy Spirit whisper.... "Thank You.")

Bible says, "To pray in The Spirit on all occasions"

Pray each day.... "Pray with tongues & pray with understanding...."

(For Study: 1 Corinthians 14)

I bless you that as you hunger & thirst....you shall be filled & that out of you will flow rivers of living water...

I bless you...to receive & be used in The Baptism of The Holy Spirit....become God's witness to the ends of the Earth & that these signs shall follow those who believe.... *"And these signs will follow those who believe: In My Name they will cast out demons; they will speak with new tongues; "They will take up serpents; and if they drink anything deadly, it will by no means hurt them; they will lay hands on the sick, and they will recover."* Mark 16:17-18, Vs. 20 says, *"And they went out and preached everywhere, The Lord working with them and confirming the word through the accompanying signs. Amen."*

I bless you to grow in The Baptism of The Holy Spirit & in your prayer language, to receive all that God has for you!

I Bless you... In Jesus Name!!

God Bless, contact us, let us know how God has touched you..... spread the fire.... Receive, Pray & Use, The Baptism of The Holy Spirit...In Jesus Name! Amen.

Ingram Content Group UK Ltd.
Milton Keynes UK
UKHW050651280323
419284UK00008B/46